Every Day with Jesus

The Pres...

'You make known to me the path of life; you will fill me with joy in your presence, with eternal pleasures at your right hand.' Psalm 16:11

Selwyn Hughes

Revised and updated by Mick Brooks

FURTHER STUDY: IAN SEWTER

© CWR 2015. Dated text previously published as *Every Day with Jesus: Experiencing God's presence* (May/June 2004) by CWR. This edition revised and updated for 2016 by Mick Brooks.

CWR, Waverley Abbey House, Waverley Lane, Farnham, Surrey GU9 8EP, UK **Tel: 01252 784700**
Email: mail@cwr.org.uk Registered Charity No. 294387. Registered Limited Company No. 1990308.

Cover image: Getty/Vincenzo Lombardo
Quiet Time image: Unsplash.com/Greg Razoky
Printed in England by Linney Print

MIX
Paper from responsible sources
FSC® C015900

A word of introduction ...

Nothing, I believe, can compare with the presence of God. I often picture the scene painted for us in Exodus 33:7-11 with Joshua, the young leader to be, lingering behind, soaking up the presence of God in the tent of meeting.

We live in a time when almost any and all information is accessible. We know a lot about a lot of things. The good news is that God wants us not just to know *about* Him but to *know* Him. Amazingly, He takes time to reveal Himself to us.

This issue was originally written out of a particular burden of Selwyn's. He grew concerned that a number of Christians he'd encountered thought that the Christian life was about 'doing' things required of us, such as reading His Word, engaging in prayer, loving our neighbours, practising Christ-like attitudes and actions in all that we do. Whilst all these things are indeed worthwhile, the most important truth to grasp hold of is that we can *know* God and *be known* by Him. We can experience the presence of God in our day-to-day lives. There are countless Christians who, although they have by faith encountered God through His Son Jesus, fail to feel or sense His ongoing presence in their lives.

This, then, is the theme we set out to explore in this issue: to practice the presence of God in our lives and learn how to experience Him more deeply. My prayer and deep desire is that these daily meditations would lead you to knowing God in the way He longs for you to know Him.

Mick Brooks, Consulting Editor

 Free small group resources to accompany this issue can be found at www.cwr.org.uk/extra. The *EDWJ* Facebook community is growing! To join the conversation visit www.facebook.com/edwjpage **f**

Experiencing God

FOR READING & MEDITATION - HEBREWS 13:1-8
'God has said, "Never will I leave you; never will I forsake you."' (v5)

Today we begin a series of meditations in which we consider how we can experience God's presence in our lives more fully. Right away it has to be said that some Christians are deeply suspicious of any emphasis on experiencing God. They regard putting emphasis on experience as spiritually dangerous on the grounds that it is likely to cause people to rely more on experience than on the written Word.

There is, of course, a danger that we will become more interested in experiences than in getting to know God through His Word, but a well-balanced, mature Christian will know God in both ways. It is important to realise that there will be times in our life when we may not be aware of God's presence as strongly as at other times – when we are sick, perhaps, or our physical condition is low – but on the basis of the text before us today we know that He is with us still. God's promise is unimpeachable – He will *never* leave us or forsake us.

How sad it is to come across Christians who never fail to read their Bibles yet have no real experience of God. One such person was heard to say, 'I have been a Christian for over twenty years, read and studied my Bible every day, but I cannot say I sense God's presence with me wherever I go. I hear other Christians say that they do and I wonder whether it is just a figment of my imagination.'

Permit me on this opening day to ask: How deeply and powerfully do you experience God in your life? How aware are you of His presence, not as a theory but as a fact? Believe me, God wants you to do more than take His presence by faith; He wants you to experience it also.

FURTHER STUDY

Gen. 28:10-16;
Deut. 31:1-6

1. What was Jacob's experience of God's presence?

2. Why can we be strong and courageous?

My Father and my God, I reach out to You on this opening day. Please help me live a balanced life. May I not only believe You are always with me but experience Your presence also. In Jesus' name. Amen.

Religion or relationship?

FOR READING & MEDITATION - JOHN 5:31-47

'You diligently study the Scriptures ... yet you refuse to come to me to have life.' (vv39-40)

I n this issue we are setting out to focus on ways in which we can increase our awareness of God's presence in our lives, hence the title of this issue: The Presence of God. Christians have the assurance that God is with them constantly and that His presence remains with them through thick and thin for, as we saw yesterday, He has promised, 'Never will I leave you; never will I forsake you' (Heb. 13:5). The words of the psalmist also make this clear: 'He keeps his eye upon you as you come and go and always guards you' (Psa. 121:8, TLB).

FURTHER STUDY

Isa. 1:10-19;
Phil. 3:3-9

1. Why are religious practices not enough?

2. How can we know God?

Honesty compels me to admit, however, that although Scripture assures us that we are constantly guarded and surrounded by the presence of God, we do not always feel that this is so. There are many possible reasons for this, as we mentioned yesterday – for instance, a poor physical condition, pain or God taking us through a wilderness experience. But let it be understood right away that if we are Christians yet do not regularly experience God's presence in our lives then we are not living in the fullness that God has designed us for.

Before we look at some of the ways in which we can increase our awareness of God's presence in our lives I feel I must say that no one can experience the continuous presence of God until he or she has come into a relationship with Him. Though the practice of religious techniques may be helpful to those who have already come to know Him, He can never be known by them alone. We get to know God in the same way that we get to know any human being – by forming a relationship with Him. No relationship, no true knowledge of God.

Heavenly Father, I must ask myself if I am simply religious or if I have a relationship with You. Help me to see that religion without a relationship leads nowhere. In Jesus' name I ask this. Amen.

'From the eternal realms'

FOR READING & MEDITATION - LUKE 15:1-7

'Suppose one of you has a hundred sheep and loses one ...
Does he not ... go after the lost sheep?' (v4)

Yesterday I highlighted the issue that before we can fully experience the presence of God we need to enter into a relationship with Him. Those who are already Christians please bear with me as I expand this point.

The answer to the question 'How do I find God?' is this: you do not have to find Him; you simply have to let Him find you. We discover in the pages of the Bible that not only do men and women search for God but that God Himself searches for them. Read the whole of Luke 15. What is Jesus telling us in the parable we have read today and the parables of the lost coin and the lost son? He is saying that the God of the universe is involved in a persistent and redemptive search for us. How amazing!

'In finding God,' Mahatma Gandhi once said, 'you must have as much patience as a man who sits by the seaside and undertakes to empty the ocean, lifting up one drop of water with a straw.' Respectfully, on this issue the great man was wrong. These parables tell us why as they fling back the curtains and let us see the God of the shepherd-heart who searches for the lost sheep until He finds it; the God who sweeps the universe with the broom of His redemptive grace until He finds the coin on which His image is stamped; the God whose love is so powerful that it lays siege to the hearts of those who have run from their Father's house. The thrilling truth is this: you do not have to search laboriously to find God in the sense of looking for Him here, there and everywhere. He is actually searching for you. And His search for you guarantees that your search for Him will result in a divine–human encounter.

FURTHER STUDY

Luke 19:1-10;
John 3:16

1. What was Jesus' message to Zacchaeus?

2. What is the message of John 3:16?

Father God, I am so glad that I do not have to search for You but just consent to be found. You have come all the way from the eternal realms to stand at the door of my heart. I dare not refuse You. My heart is open, Lord Jesus. Come in. Amen.

Consent – the key

FOR READING & MEDITATION – JAMES 4:1-10
'Come near to God and he will come near to you.' (v8)

At present we are looking at one of the greatest truths in the universe, namely that God is on a persistent redemptive search for us. We are seeing that entering into a relationship with God is not so much a matter of trying to find Him as of letting Him find us. This is not understood, however, to mean that since God has done everything possible to save us our individual salvation is now automatic. God has gone to the utmost lengths to save us, but in order to know Him we need to now turn to Him in contrition and repentance and invite Him to take up residence within us.

FURTHER STUDY

Luke 15:11-24; John 1:12; Rev. 3:20

1. What did the son do to experience his father's presence?

2. What must we do?

I have met many people who thought that because they felt God close to them at certain times in their life (for instance, when they had a miraculous escape from death or something happened that seemed more than a coincidence) they must have been favoured by Him and had no need to invite Him into their hearts. I have no doubt that many people have an awareness of God's presence at times, but they can never fully experience the rich sense of His presence in their hearts until they invite Him to come in. He loves every one of His creation, but He loves them too much to gatecrash the soul. He comes in only as we give our consent.

'No one is constitutionally incapable of finding God,' says E. Stanley Jones. If we do not find Him then the problem is not to do with our constitution but with our consent. When, by an act of the will, you decide to let God in then, believe me, nothing in earth or heaven can keep Him out. So if you realise that what you have is religion and not a personal relationship with God then pray this prayer with me now:

Gracious and loving Father, I realise that my eternal destiny is in my own hands. You have done all You need to do, so now I must do what I need to do. Loving Father, I come. Please save me. In Jesus' name I ask it. Amen.

If you prayed this prayer for the first time and would like a copy of Selwyn's booklet *Every Day with Jesus for New Christians*, please write to CWR.

CWR Ministry Events

PLEASE PRAY FOR THE TEAM

E	EVENT	PLACE	PRESENTER(S)
y	Great Chapters of the Bible: Great is Your Faithfulness	Waverley Abbey House	Philip Greenslade
y	Transformed by the love of the Father	WAH	Liz Babbs
ay	Christ Empowered Living	WAH	Mick and Lynette Brooks
ay	Small Groups Rebooted	WAH	Andy Peck
0 May	May Country Break	Pilgrim Hall	Pilgrim Hall Team
ay	Church Leaders' Forum	WAH	Andy Peck and Pete Greig
1; 8 May	Counselling Certificate, Module 2	Singapore	Ron Kallmier and Anna Clarkstone
6 May	Counselling Certificate, Module 2	Cambodia	Ron Kallmier and Anna Clarkstone
Jun	Partners' Break	PH	CWR Team
4 Jun	Bible Discovery Weekend: Vital Connections	WAH	Philip Greenslade
24 Jun	Introduction to Biblical Care and Counselling	PH	John Munt and Team
un	Ten things to know about the Old Testament (evening)	WAH	Philip Greenslade
Jun	IWED Summer Day: 'Give it A Rest'	WAH	Judy Moore
un	Ten things to know about the New Testament (evening)	WAH	Philip Greenslade

Please pray for our students and tutors on our ongoing BA Counselling programme at Waverley Abbey House and Pilgrim Hall, as well as our Certificate and Diploma of Christian Counselling and MA in Christian Counselling qualifications.

We would also appreciate prayer for our ongoing ministry in Singapore as well as our many regional events that we are embarking on this year.

For further information and a full list of CWR's courses, phone **+44 (0)1252 784719** or visit the CWR website **www.cwr.org.uk**

You can also download our free daily Prayer Track from **www.cwr.org.uk/free-resources**

'Turn strong to meet the day'

FOR READING & MEDITATION - PSALM 139:13-18
'When I awake, I am still with you.' (v18)

This psalm is so helpful in expressing how we can experience God's presence all the time, that I will be referring to it a few more times in this issue. Now that we are clear that we cannot experience the full, ongoing presence of God until He resides within us, we are ready to begin considering some of the things we can do in order to become more conscious of His indwelling presence.

So much of the news can induce fear and helplessness in us if that's all we allow to fill our minds. We can learn to be more aware of what we *do* have rather than what we don't have. So my first suggestion is this: as you awake each morning, turn to God in an attitude of spiritual expectancy. A friend of mine says that this suggestion, which was given to him in the early days of his Christian experience, has been the chief means of sharpening the sense of God's presence in his life. Listen to these words written by an unknown poet:

FURTHER STUDY

Psa. 119:145-152;
Mark 1:29-37

1. What was the psalmist's practice?

2. What was Jesus' example?

Every morning lean thine arm awhile
Upon the window sill of heaven
And gaze upon thy God;
Then with the vision in thy heart
Turn strong to meet the day.

'Turn strong to meet the day.' What an optimistic thought! And why not? Anyone who looks into the face of God is fortified and prepared to deal with anything the day may bring.

Someone has commented that there are two kinds of Christians: those who wake up in the morning, look around the room and say rather gloomily, 'Oh Lord, another day,' and those who wake up, look into their heavenly Father's face and say with energy and expectation, 'Oh Lord, another day!' Which kind, I wonder, are you?

Father, help me to begin every day by looking into Your face before I look into anyone else's. Then, with the vision of You in my heart, I too will be able to 'turn strong to meet the day'. Amen.

'Good morning, Lord!'

FOR READING & MEDITATION - PSALM 108:1-13

'Awake, harp and lyre! I will awaken the dawn.' (v2)

Today we think a little more about the importance of turning to God in the first few moments after we awake in an attitude of spiritual expectancy. Those who study the effect of thought upon the personality suggest that our last thought at night determines to a large degree the quality of our sleep and our first thought in the morning influences our attitudes to life. We shall consider the significance of our last thought at night a little later on, and think now about focusing our waking thoughts on God.

How will this help? It helps by giving a divine perspective to the day. If your day begins with God it is more likely to continue and end with Him. The way in which we start determines to a large degree the way in which we continue and the way we finish. A number of Christians say that their awareness of the fact that God is with them is increased by turning to Him as soon as they are awake and saying, 'Good morning, Lord.' Sentimental? Some might think so, but one of the many things I have learned in my Christian life is that what suits one does not necessarily suit another. The method you use to focus your thoughts on God in the moments after you awake is not important; what is important is that your thoughts turn away from your own self and are directed instead to God.

A friend of mine once said, 'Every morning, as I awake, I lie there in my bed for a few moments and tell myself, "When I open my eyes, the light comes in; when I open my mouth, the air comes in; when I open my heart, Christ comes in."' Such thoughts help to prime the pump of the soul and cause the water of life to spring upwards into the day.

FURTHER STUDY

Exod. 29:38-46; 30:7;
1 Sam. 1:10-19

1. What did the priests do each morning?

2. What did Hannah do in the morning?

Lord God, help me to begin each day by opening every pore, every cell, every tissue, every artery, every part of my being to You. In Jesus' name I pray. Amen.

'Naturalised in defeat'

FOR READING & MEDITATION – PSALM 62:1-12

'Find rest, O my soul, in God alone; my hope comes from him.' (v5)

We continue reflecting on what we can do to increase our sense of God's presence in our lives and how we can go about sharpening our spiritual sensitivity. One of the very first things we can do, we are saying, is to look to Him in an attitude of spiritual expectancy as soon as we awake in the morning. Please notice the phrase 'an attitude of spiritual expectancy'. As we awake we can remind ourselves that God is with us and will be with us through every hour of the day.

A matter that deeply saddens me is the spirit of non-expectancy that I occasionally encounter amongst groups of Christians. When believers do not expect anything spiritually exciting to happen during the day they limit themselves; expecting nothing more than to just be able to muddle through. This is serious. If you consider certain worldviews and philosophies, you can see how they affect entire cultures. Whenever I come across this somewhat sad attitude, I find otherwise lovely people responding fatalistically to situations by turning over their hands in an attitude of helpless resignation.

FURTHER STUDY

Num. 13:27-14:4,20-24

1. How were the Israelites naturalised in defeat?

2. What was the expectation of Caleb?

The same danger lies at the door of the contemporary Christian Church. In some cases it has actually crossed the threshold and started to paralyse the hearts of God's people, causing them to become resigned to simply live with a defeatist and hang tight attitude. A medical practitioner who has worked in clinics among people who are troubled both in body and soul, says, 'Most Christians do not expect their religion to do them any great or immediate good. They have become naturalised in defeat. They get nothing from God because they expect nothing from God.' How sad.

Heavenly Father, help me to become an expectant person. Teach me how to go into every day as relaxed and receptive as a little child. Then life will take on a new perspective and my hardest tasks become pure joy. In Jesus' name I ask it. Amen.

'Faith – largely expectancy'

FOR READING & MEDITATION - ISAIAH 30:15-26
'Yet the LORD longs to be gracious to you; he rises to show you compassion.' (v18)

Yesterday we said that some Christians begin their day in a spirit of non-expectancy. They expect nothing spiritually exciting or profitable to happen to them – and that is mostly what occurs. Such people think it utterly inconceivable that God should want to speak to them, guide them or reveal Himself to them in some new and fresh way; they regard such experiences as being strange and abnormal. The Amplified Bible translates today's text in this way: 'And therefore the Lord [earnestly] waits [expecting, looking and longing] to be gracious to you'. If the Lord looks at us with expectancy then can we not look to Him in the same way? How wonderful it would be if our expectancy could match His!

A story I have told before concerns a little girl who was unable to walk upright and straight as a result of a disability. After lengthy treatment she began to walk straight. The first time she did so she burst into tears, threw herself into her mother's arms, and cried, 'Oh Mummy, I'm walking all crooked!' Christians who lack a spirit of expectancy are like that – they think that walking through the day with their heads held high and a song in their hearts is something that feels strange and out of their reach.

'Faith,' said Dr Cynddylan Jones, a famous Welsh preacher, 'is largely expectancy – expectancy set on fire by the Holy Spirit.' I promise you that if you begin your day by looking into your heavenly Father's face in a spirit of expectancy you will not be disappointed. Learn to push expectantly on the gates of abundant living as you awake each morning and, as surely as day follows night, those gates will open wide.

FURTHER STUDY

Matt. 8:5-13; 9:18-30; 17:20-21

1. How did people show expectancy?

2. How much faith do we need?

Lord God, if faith is 'expectancy set on fire by the Holy Spirit' then breathe upon the embers of my heart today so that my whole being shall be set aflame – aflame with expectancy. In Jesus' name I ask this. Amen.

Cultivating closeness

FOR READING & MEDITATION - LAMENTATIONS 3:22-36
'the LORD's ... compassions never fail. They are new every morning'
(vv22-23)

The renowned Anglican preacher and author John Stott said that every morning when he rose from his bed he turned his thoughts to God and uttered these words: 'Good morning heavenly Father, good morning Lord Jesus, good morning Holy Spirit.' His very first focus in the morning was on the Trinity. It is a practice I would commend.

When I was a child a prayer written by Henry Van Dyke hung on the wall of my bedroom. Every morning when I awoke I saw these words and they burned themselves into my memory:

FURTHER STUDY

Deut. 6:1-9;
Psa. 119:9-16

1. Where should we put God's Word?

2. How did God's Word affect the psalmist?

Ere thou risest from thy bed,
Speak to God whose wings were spread,
O'er thee in the helpless night.
Lo, He wakes thee now with light,
Lift thy burden and thy care,
In the mighty arms of prayer.

It is sad, I think, that nowadays the majority of Christian homes do not display prayers, mottos or spiritual sayings such as this. In my home I have a plaque that reads, 'in this place will I give peace, saith the LORD of hosts' (Hag. 2:9, KJV). When my wife was dying, she would look at that plaque and say, 'I feel pain but I also feel His peace.'

For many years, there sat a wooden carving of the word 'Jesus' on top of my TV. When I received the news of my second son's death, I was overcome with grief. It was hard to pray, at first I was so stunned and shocked, but, as I looked up, I saw the name of Jesus on that carving. His name was the only prayer I could pray – and He became a place of refuge and strength. We should do all that we can do to remind ourselves of God's promises and of His presence.

Lord Jesus, help me to begin each day with You, I pray. Drive deep within my soul the truth that You are the most important person in my life, and for that reason my first contact in the morning should be with You. In Your name. Amen.

Give a gift to
the next generation

By leaving a legacy gift to CWR in your will you could help us provide Bible reading notes to enable the next generation to understand and apply God's Word to their lives.

Inspire others as they live every day with Jesus, applying His Word to their lives, every day. With your help, we can help children as they grow in their relationship with God through our youth titles, develop initiatives to help people engage with the Bible in new ways and reach even more people through the development of new courses that will impact the Church and society.

After considering your loved ones, a gift to CWR will make a lasting impact on the lives of our brothers and sisters around the world. By leaving a legacy to CWR you will share your passion for Bible reading with others – a gift motivated by your heart for God's Word to inspire the next generation.

If you would like further information, please email **legacy@cwr.org.uk** or call **01252 784709**.

The divine exchange

FOR READING & MEDITATION – PSALM 5:1-12

'In the morning, O LORD, you hear my voice; in the morning I lay my requests before you' (v3)

What an amazing picture today's text paints for our faith: God eagerly waiting for us to awake, listening for our voice. Many other verses in the psalms also describe this interaction – God's attentiveness to us and our attentiveness to Him. The New Jerusalem Bible has a particularly wonderful translation of this text: 'To you I pray, Yahweh, At daybreak you hear my voice; at daybreak I lay my case before you and fix my eyes on you.'

One of the difficulties in the Church today is that many Christians do not spend enough time reading their Bible. Is it any wonder that spiritually speaking they are running on empty? I cannot conceive of any Christian having read today's verse not wanting to put it into practice, that is, lifting one's voice to God in praise and thankfulness the moment one is awake.

FURTHER STUDY

Exod. 16:11-21;
Luke 21:37-38

1. What were the Israelites to do each morning?

2. What did the Jews do in the morning?

This verse is recorded in Scripture, I believe, not simply to show us how one particular person – the psalmist – conducted his devotional life, but also to give us a principle to follow. Scripture contains many such images that remind us that God is watching over us and longing to engage with us. The psalms are particularly rich in this regard. For instance, Psalm 121 tells us that He never sleeps and never gets tired. Our being attentive to Him is not the reason that He is attentive to us, but when we give ourselves to Him we become increasingly conscious of His loving, constant watchfulness over us.

Nothing I know of is more wonderful than the realisation that God eagerly holds Himself in readiness to engage with us as soon as we awake. May we eagerly hold ourselves in readiness for Him.

Father God, may I be as eager to engage with You when I awake as You are to engage with me. During the first moments of every morning may there be a divine exchange – You meeting with me and me meeting with You. In Jesus' name. Amen.

The quiet time

FOR READING & MEDITATION - PSALM 88:1-18

'But I cry to you for help, O LORD; in the morning my prayer comes before you.' (v13)

The second measure I would like to suggest as we consider ways in which we can increase our awareness of our Lord's presence in our daily life is this: establish a time, as soon as possible after you awake, when you can be alone with Him in prayer and contemplation. I know of nothing that sharpens the awareness of God's presence in a believer's life more powerfully and effectively than the regular practice of a morning quiet time.

Nowadays the term 'quiet time' is regarded by many as old-fashioned, and, to our shame, the practice of setting time aside to be alone with God is deemed to be unrealistic because life is so busy. Yet I have found that those who do not have a quiet time are more likely to have an unquiet time during the day. Whether or not you use the term 'quiet time', try to start the day by spending a little time with God. If you do not then I believe you are missing out. This is the reason why in Scripture there are so many references to beginning the day with God.

A favourite story of mine is that of Susannah Wesley, the godly mother of John Wesley, who had many children to care for and was therefore deprived of privacy for her quiet time. For a few minutes each morning she would lift her apron over her head and commune in prayer with God. When the children saw this they would whisper to each other, 'Hush, mother is having her quiet time.' Do what you can to be alone when you have your quiet time. Married couples should pray together regularly but one's quiet time is best spent alone with God. Savour the moments you spend with Him at the start of the day – they will provide you with a fountain of life-giving water throughout the day.

FURTHER STUDY

Psa. 130:1-8;
Matt. 6:6;
Luke 5:16

1. What was Jesus' regular habit?

2. Why is it important to be alone with God?

My Father and my God, help me to see that although You live within my heart I must not take You for granted. My awareness of You will depend on how often I make contact with You. Help me to cultivate a greater closeness. In Jesus' name. Amen.

Take it!

FOR READING & MEDITATION - PSALM 55:1-23

'Evening, morning and noon I cry out in distress, and he hears my voice.' (v17)

Today we continue focusing on the importance of establishing a time, soon after we have awakened, when we can cultivate a closeness with Jesus and sharpen our awareness of His presence in our lives. In all my years as a Christian I have never met anyone who experienced a deep and constant sense of God's presence yet did not have regular times of prayer and contemplation.

Sadly, some I have met have told me that after being baptised in the Holy Spirit they felt such a keen sense of God in their lives that they no longer needed to set aside certain times to spend with Him in prayer. As I have mentioned before, one man put it like this: 'Before I was filled with the Spirit I used to have some pretty dull quiet times. Now I have an ongoing "quiet time" that lasts every moment I am awake. I no longer need to get alone with God in prayer or spend much time reading the Bible. I am more alive to God than I ever thought was possible.' I warned this man what would happen if he neglected fixed times with the Lord, and it was no surprise to hear a few months later that his relationship with God had become cold, indifferent and distant.

FURTHER STUDY

Matt. 26:41;
Luke 18:1-8;
Eph. 6:18-20

1. What truth does the parable teach?

2. Why should we pray?

Those who say that they can live in a state of strong spiritual awareness without having definite times for prayer and contemplation will probably find that eventually they neglect both. And to do so is like saying that one can live in a state of physical nourishment without eating regularly. Setting time aside to cultivate an awareness of God results in us enjoying a continual awareness of God. You can take the habit or leave it, but believe me, life works best when you take it.

Lord God, teach me to find the time for daily prayer and contemplation, for I see that the benefits far exceed the difficulties I may experience in establishing it. For Jesus' sake. Amen.

The best way to begin

FOR READING & MEDITATION - PSALM 119:97-112

'Your word is a lamp to my feet and a light for my path.' (v105)

Yesterday we said that some feel they can enjoy a constant sense of God's presence without making time for prayer and contemplation. The New Testament shows us that Jesus felt the need for three simple habits: (1) He went into the synagogue to read, 'as was his custom' (Luke 4:16); (2) He frequently went up a mountain to pray (see, for example, Matt. 14:23; Luke 6:12); (3) He taught the people daily (Matt. 26:55). These three simple habits – reading the Scriptures, spending time in prayer and sharing with others – are as basic to the Christian life as 'two and two make four' is to mathematics. If Jesus made this His practice, what better model is there?

So how can we make the best of our daily or regular times of prayer and contemplation? There can be no fixed rules – only suggestions. I believe morning is best, but later in the day may work for you. Whenever you do it, experience has shown that the best way to begin is by reading the Scriptures. This is the reason why, many years ago, I began writing *Every Day with Jesus*. Prior to that, whenever I advised people to begin their quiet time by reading the Word of God, they would to say, 'But I don't know what to read.' You cannot realise the joy it gives me to know that thousands of people who previously had no daily quiet time now begin their day by reading the Word of God, and then use these devotional thoughts. My words, as I have said before, help many, but they are not one-millionth as powerful and effective as the words of God through the Scriptures. Life speaks to life. God has inspired the writing of His Word and so, when we read it, God speaks to us through the words.

FURTHER STUDY

Psa. 19:7-14; Heb. 4:12

1. What does God's Word accomplish?

2. Why is it so powerful?

Father, I am so thankful for the Scriptures and for the inspiration and power that flows through them. Help me to love Your Word and delight daily in it. For Your own dear name's sake. Amen.

Who speaks the most?

FOR READING & MEDITATION - 1 SAMUEL 3:1-19
'say, "Speak, LORD, for your servant is listening."' (v9)

How then can we make the best of our quiet time? Another suggestion is that after reading the Bible you should sit quietly in the Lord's presence and ask, 'Father, have You anything to say to me?' Sometimes God may have something special and personal to say to you arising from your reading of His Word. Wait and see what He might have to say to you before moving on. One lady who once practiced this approach told me that when she asks, 'Father, have You anything to say to me?' the Lord sometimes responds, 'No, nothing more than I have already said in My Word. But what have you to say to Me?'

FURTHER STUDY

Prov. 8:32-36;
James 1:19

1. What happens when we listen to God's wisdom?

2. What is James' advice?

God not only delights in talking to us but He is delighted also when we talk to Him. This is what prayer is – an authentic relationship with God. So talk to Him. Tell Him the things that are on your mind – the joyful *and* difficult things. If your mind wanders or gets distracted then pray about the thing to which your mind has wandered. Before writing these notes, while I was at prayer, I was distracted by the siren of an ambulance so I prayed, 'Lord, whatever the problem is that has sent this ambulance racing through the streets, be there to help and guide.' The distraction became a direction. This is maybe what Paul meant when he said that we 'take captive every thought to make it obedient to Christ' (2 Cor. 10:5).

Here is another suggestion: have a notebook and a pen near at hand in case God says something specific to you that you'll want to remember. If I had not written down what came to me during my quiet times over the years then I would definitely have missed out. A notebook can be a sign of faith; it shows that we are expecting God to speak.

Lord God, forgive me that so often my prayer life is conducted in the attitude of 'Listen, Lord, Your servant is speaking' rather than 'Speak, Lord, Your servant is listening.' Help me to change things - starting today. Amen.

Who cares?

Many of us go through difficult times, such as the uncertainty of illness, bereavement or being made redundant, without help or support from someone who really understand the stress, isolation and fear we are facing.

But what if there *was* someone nearby who understood? What if there were people in the Church who had gone through something very similar? They could do more than just understand; in fact, their experience, their journey and their breakthroughs could really help and support us through, so that we too could come out the other side.

CWR's new six-week initiative, **Paraclesis: Journeying Together** written by Trevor J. Partridge, encourages pastoral care at a ground roots level and offers the Church a new opportunity to journey alongside people, the way that God journeys alongside us.

Following successful pilot projects in a number of churches around the world, Paraclesis: Journeying Together is now available for churches to embark on together, sharing their life experience in a structured and supportive way.

By adopting Paraclesis in your church and coming alongside others, together we can respond to those in our congregations and communities who are thinking 'Who cares?' with the answer, 'We care'.

paraclesis
Coming alongside others

Sign up now to learn more about Paraclesis, purchase resources and receive a starter pack, so you and your church can begin your care journey together. Visit our website **www.paraclesis.org.uk** for more information.

The Spirit makes Christ real

FOR READING & MEDITATION - EPHESIANS 5:8-20

'Do not get drunk on wine, which leads to debauchery.
Instead, be filled with the Spirit.' (v18)

We are continuing our consideration of the options that are open to us for increasing our awareness of the presence of God in our lives. I use the word 'options' because we can choose either to take them or leave them; God will not force them upon us. He makes Himself available to us, and when we make ourselves available to Him we will find that we have a deep and continuous sense of His presence in our hearts.

Another way, then, in which we can heighten the awareness of God's presence with us is, as our text puts it, to 'be filled with the Spirit'. This is a wonderful text to consider on this Pentecost Sunday. One of the ministries of the Holy Spirit is to make God and His Son, Jesus Christ, known to us: 'He [the Holy Spirit] will bring glory to me by taking from what is mine and making it known to you' (John 16:14). It follows, therefore, that the more we allow the Holy Spirit to have sway in our lives, the more aware we will be of the divine presence.

FURTHER STUDY

Acts 2:1-6,14-21

1. What happened when people were filled with the Holy Spirit?

2. What was the reaction of the crowd?

Now the question will be asked: What does it mean to be filled with the Spirit? Does not every Christian possess the Holy Spirit? The answer is 'Yes', for Scripture teaches that every Christian has the Holy Spirit from the moment of their conversion. Take this verse, for example: 'I tell you the truth, no-one can enter the kingdom of God unless he is born of water and the Spirit' (John 3:5). However, although every Christian has the Holy Spirit, the Holy Spirit does not have every Christian in the sense that they do not allow Him to fill every part of their lives. In the light of this, can I ask you to face this question with me before going any further: I have the Holy Spirit, but does He really have me?

Father God, help me not to evade this question. You have given all of Yourself to me - please help me give all of myself to You. In Jesus' name I pray. Amen.

FOR READING & MEDITATION - JOHN 14:15-27

'But you know him, for he lives with you and will be in you.' (v17)

If, as we saw yesterday, every Christian has the Holy Spirit, then why is there an ongoing debate among Christians about such matters as 'the baptism of the Spirit', 'being filled with the Spirit' and 'walking in the Spirit'? In the early days of my Christian experience I thought long and hard about the gift of the Holy Spirit, but it was not until I understood the three different prepositions that Jesus used in relation to the Spirit that the matter became clearer to me. Someone has said, 'A preposition can alter a proposition,' and nowhere is that more true than in relation to the teaching and understanding of the ministry of the Holy Spirit in our lives. Get your prepositions right and you will have no difficulty with the propositions. The three prepositions that Jesus used when talking about the Holy Spirit are these: 'with', 'in' and 'on'. Let's look at each of these in turn.

FURTHER STUDY

John 3:5-8;
15:26; 16:7-15

1. What does the Holy Spirit do for us?

2. Why was it good for Jesus to go away?

What did Jesus mean when He said the Holy Spirit was 'with' the disciples? He meant, so I believe, that the Spirit was accompanying them, was working with them from the outside. He most certainly was not in them for Jesus clearly indicated that that phase of the Spirit's work would start at some point in the future. We see this from the words found in today's text: 'he … will be in you.'

This is how the Spirit worked in our lives prior to our conversion. He was with us in order to convict us of sin and reveal to us the true nature and character of Jesus – and our relationships and standing with Him. Wonderful and awesome though it may be to have the Spirit with us, there can be no real radical transformation in our lives until the Holy Spirit moves within us.

Father, how can I sufficiently thank You for the change Your Spirit has brought about in my life since the day You came in? If I want anything more, it is more of what I have. Amen.

The disciples and the Spirit

FOR READING & MEDITATION - JOHN 20:19-31

'And with that he breathed on them and said,
"Receive the Holy Spirit."' (v22)

Yesterday we ended with the statement 'Wonderful and awesome though it may be to have the Spirit with us, there can be no real radical transformation in our lives until the Holy Spirit moves within us.' This brings us to the question: When did the disciples experience the Holy Spirit 'in their lives' to regenerate them and bring them into the fullness of new birth?

Many people will say that this took place on the Day of Pentecost. I do not think so myself, and let me explain why here. Our passage today depicts that glorious post-resurrection meeting of Jesus with His disciples when, after commissioning them, He proceeded to breathe on them, saying as He did so, 'Receive the Holy Spirit.' I believe that was the moment they received the Holy Spirit in their lives. But if that is so, then what happened on the Day of Pentecost? Was that a double portion of the Spirit? This is where our prepositions can really help to explain things. Here in the locked room, so I believe, the disciples' hearts were regenerated and transformed by the Holy Spirit. He who had been 'with' them now came 'in' them to convert them.

Although the disciples belonged to Jesus before the crucifixion and resurrection, they could not have experienced the regenerative power of the Spirit, for that could only have been generously given to them following Jesus' death and resurrection and His overcoming the grave. It is interesting that Jesus' first act when meeting His disciples after coming back from the dead is to impart to them the Holy Spirit. Now, because of the crucifixion and resurrection, He who had been *with* them was able to come *into* them.

FURTHER STUDY

Gen. 2:7;
Psa. 33:6;
Ezek. 37:1-14

1. What does the breath of God accomplish?

2. What happened when God's breath met the presence of death?

Heavenly Father, once again I bow before You in deepest gratitude for the fact that Your Spirit is not just 'with' me but 'in' me. These are just little words, dear Lord, but they mean big things. I am so grateful. Amen.

The Day of Pentecost

FOR READING & MEDITATION - ACTS 1:1-14

'But you will receive power when the Holy Spirit comes on you' (v8)

Now we look at the third preposition Jesus used in relation to the Holy Spirit, which is found in today's text: 'You will receive power when the Holy Spirit comes on you.' This was a prophetic reference to a day not far distant – the Day of Pentecost – when the Spirit would start to play a different part in their lives. So now we must ask ourselves: What happened at Pentecost?

The Holy Spirit who had been 'with' the disciples prior to the crucifixion and resurrection and came 'in' them following the resurrection would now come 'on' them in all His fullness to saturate them with divine power and turn them from timid, vacillating, hidden disciples into men and women who were ablaze and very visible. And did that happen? Let the facts speak for themselves. When the Spirit came in fullness at Pentecost the disciples who hitherto, though converted and committed to Jesus, had been somewhat frightened and dispirited, began to feel His personal presence in a way that transformed them within. Now they had no doubt that Jesus was actually living in their lives and, feeling His personal presence with them, they went out and began to turn the world upside down.

What has all this to do with what we are saying? This – although the Spirit has been 'with' you in order to bring you to Jesus and is now 'in' you through the work of regeneration and transformation, the question remains: Have you experienced your own personal Pentecost and do you know the Spirit clothing you, enduing you with divine energy and power? Whatever your view of the Holy Spirit, it is essential that you ask: Is He dynamic or merely a doctrine?

FURTHER STUDY

Acts 4:31; 10:44-48; 19:1-6

1. What were the results of the Holy Spirit coming upon people?

2. Why were the circumcised believers astonished?

Lord God, save me from being satisfied with just an intellectual understanding of the doctrine of the Spirit. Here, where I am now, please give me what You gave those first 120 disciples. In Jesus' name. Amen.

'Your senior partner'

FOR READING & MEDITATION - JOHN 15:1-11
'Remain in me, and I will remain in you.' (v4)

Now we move on to consider another suggestion we can explore in order to increase our awareness of God's presence in our lives: order your day on the basis of a divine partnership.

This idea is one that I was given many years ago by an elderly Welsh miner. He said to me that every day, following his quiet time, he would think of what he had to do that day and then would actively visualise Jesus as being involved in every moment of it. 'I am in partnership with God,' he said, 'and I have learned to think of the responsibilities of the day not as "mine" but as "ours".' He went on to tell me that as he thought ahead about the issues that would arise during the day he would talk to God about them in the same way that a man would talk to a business partner: 'What shall we do about this matter, Lord? There's another issue that will be coming up later in the day … how shall we handle that? And then there is that other matter that just has to be completed today … we need to be particularly careful about that, Father. How shall we deal with it?'

The chief merit of this approach is that it highlights one of the greatest truths of Scripture, namely that it is possible for us to enter in a divine–human partnership. How wonderful it is to realise that the Almighty God, the Creator of the universe, takes an active interest in every single detail of our lives and is willing to team up with us. 'Christianity,' said a missionary who worked in China, 'is walking and working each day with a senior partner.' It is. Please always remember this: you do not need to go through any day alone, but can walk arm in arm with your senior partner.

FURTHER STUDY

Mark 16:20;
Rom. 8:12-21

1. How did God's partnership with the disciples work?

2. What do we share with Jesus?

Father God, help me to see every day not from my perspective but from *our* perspective. Without You I do not want to take one step over the threshold. But with You - I can go anywhere. Amen.

'Open secrets'

FOR READING & MEDITATION – PSALM 32:1-11

'I will instruct you and teach you in the way you should go;
I will counsel you' (v8)

We continue meditating on the thought that we can order our day on the basis of a divine partnership. Some struggle with this idea on the grounds that it makes us over-dependent and prevents us from developing as persons. 'God,' they say, 'has designed us to think for ourselves, and if we depend on Him to do our thinking for us we will not become free, self-determining, creative individuals.'

There is some truth in this argument, of course, but as so often happens, if we take just one part of a truth and do not consider the other parts we will reach the wrong conclusions. Truth out of balance becomes error. Partnership with God does not mean that He dominates us; His purpose is to guide, as we see from today's text. He never overrides. He relates to us in a way that is helpful and supportive yet, at the same time, He never suppresses our initiative and creativity. This is how E. Stanley Jones described the divine–human partnership: 'God comes close to His children in a way that leaves them free to think and act, yet in a way that awakens the personality to aliveness and alertness of mind and spirit. His guidance is always sufficiently obvious to be found, but not so obvious that it does away with the necessity of thought and discriminating insight.' God's secrets are always 'open secrets' – open, yet sufficiently secret to make us think.

This kind of partnership, which results in us being guided but not overridden, is something that divine wisdom accomplishes. We would not expect anything less of the God who loves us – and anything else would be unworthy of Him.

FURTHER STUDY

Gen. 1:26-30; 2:8-20

1. What was God's guidance to Adam?

2. What was Adam free to do and how did he and God work as partners?

Gracious Father, I am so glad that You love me in a way that does not dominate me but develops me. You guide but do not override. I am so very grateful. Amen.

Learning for life

People helping has always been at the heart of our ministry here at CWR. Over the last 30 years, we have pioneered and developed expertise in the area of Christian counselling training. More recently, Waverley Abbey College was established to provide a higher educational arm to CWR, where we continue to develop and run our academic programmes.

Alongside a Christian worldview, the Waverley Integrative Framework is a unique Christian framework, which underpins all of our teaching.

Now firmly established, the College offers both short and long term programmes, from teaching the very foundations of counselling, through to Higher Education Programmes such as our BA (Hons) in Counselling, our MA in Counselling and our MA in Relational Counselling and Psychotherapy programmes, which are currently validated by the University of Roehampton.

All of our tutors are trained counsellors who, along with a dedicated academic support team, work together to continually develop and deliver programmes that maintain academic standards and enhance the quality of student learning wherever possible. By running our programmes as part-time learning, we are also able to offer a flexible way for students to fit studying around their other commitments.

WAVERLEY ABBEY
COLLEGE

Originally, Waverley Abbey House was the location for our training. However, growing student numbers and the popularity of our courses means that Pilgrim Hall now provides the College with the capacity needed to meet the demand for greater availability for accommodation and teaching space.

With over 250 students graduated from Waverley Abbey College, many of whom now work in counselling and pastoral care positions, we look forward to our continued growth and development in helping people learn for life.

For more information on Waverley Abbey College and to order a prospectus, please visit **www.waverleyabbeycollege.ac.uk** or call **01252 784731**.

We have recently welcomed our new Director of Higher Education, Dr Andrew Hartropp to the College. Do pray for Andrew as he leads this area of our ministry forward.

Blocked channels

FOR READING & MEDITATION - JOB 31:1-12

'If I have walked in falsehood or my foot has hurried after deceit –
let God weigh me in honest scales' (vv5-6)

We have already made the observation that we can learn to partner with God daily. We can, however, block this partnership if we do not allow God to make us aware of any issues that prevent Him coming through to us, such as impurity, pride or resentment. Watch the tendency to pass over such matters as if they were not there. When we do so we are allowing our inner defences to keep us from facing things that are uncomfortable. Never defend yourself in the presence of God, either overtly or covertly. God won't get angry with you because there are blocked channels in your life. He will put His loving arms around you and help you unblock them – if you let Him. So acknowledge anything that is wrong, ask God for forgiveness and tell Him that with His help you will make matters right.

FURTHER STUDY

Exod. 20:18-21;
Psa. 85:1-13

1. Why should we not be afraid of our partner God?

2. What is the difference between relaxed respect and tense fear?

It is important to remember that God is always ready to partner with you in order to make you the best you can be. The operative word in this exercise is *relax*. Being relaxed helps us be more open to God. Many Christians, I find, are so afraid that God is going to be angry with them that they are not open to Him, and when He tries to speak to them their own tensions block out the sound of His voice. Most often this problem is caused by a wrong concept of God. Your view of God will determine the way you relate to Him. Many a person has failed to benefit in their relationship with God because they were afraid to open up to Him out of fear that they would become an object of His wrath.

God has to discipline us, of course, when we stray from His ways, but His discipline is always *loving* discipline. Every loving parent will occasionally say 'no'. His reproofs are gentle. Never forget that. Never.

Lord God, if there any blocked channels in my life please help me unblock them right now. I am so grateful that You love me enough to insist on my dealing with them. Thank You Father. Amen.

What kind of partner is God?

FOR READING & MEDITATION – HEBREWS 2:5-18

'Since the children have flesh and blood, he too shared
in their humanity ... ' (v14)

If we are to start every day on the basis of a divine–human partnership then it might be helpful to think for a moment about the way in which God fulfils this role.

One question we might ask ourselves is: Can the eternal God really understand the pressures of living in the realm of time? Is He really able to enter into our feelings and experiences? The answer, of course, is, I believe, 'Yes'. In the person of His Son, God has worn our flesh, measured its frailty and knows and understands how we think and feel. There is no need to wonder what kind of partner God makes, as all you have to do is to look at Jesus to find out. He is 'the radiance of God's glory and the exact representation of his being' (Heb. 1:3). We are also told in Hebrews 4 that He is able to sympathise with our weaknesses because He faced the same temptations and difficulties as we do (vv15–16). Let's therefore look together at some of the characteristics that Jesus, our divine partner, demonstrated when He lived on earth, and see how perfectly able He is to fulfil the role.

First, He was a person of immense courage – not the excited, desperate courage of the battlefield, but the quiet courage that persevered in the face of growing political, social and religious opposition and certain crucifixion. Does it look as if the day ahead will demand special courage and determination from you? Are you facing a situation that requires greater strength and confidence than you feel you are capable of? Then take heart: in Jesus you have a partner who knows how you feel and will, if you ask Him, release His quiet courage and determination deep into your soul this very hour.

FURTHER STUDY

Heb. 4:14-5:10;
1 Pet. 2:21-23

1. Why was it important for Jesus to be fully human?

2. What does this mean for us?

Lord Jesus Christ, my Saviour and my partner, release Your courage and confidence into the very fabric of my being so that I shall have the determination to do what has to be done. For Your own dear name's sake I ask it. Amen.

What better partner?

FOR READING & MEDITATION – PSALM 73:13-28

'Whom have I in heaven but you? And earth has nothing I desire besides you.' (v25)

We continue asking ourselves: What kind of a partner is God? Can the great Creator of the universe really understand what goes on in the hearts and minds of finite human beings? The good news is that, through the incarnate Jesus, He does. However difficult our day might be, we have in Jesus a Saviour and a partner who knows and understands our deepest needs and, what is more, He is able to provide the exact measure of strength and courage we require to meet what lies ahead.

Let's think for a moment about some of the other ways in which He reveals Himself to be the perfect partner. He cares! When He was here on earth, He cared more about the needs of others than He did about His own needs (see John 4:34). His care went beyond race, class or colour. He gives! When people consider entering into partnership with someone they usually want to know how much their partner is willing to give. But the ultimate test of partnership is not the giving of time, money, words or the willingness to attend meetings but the giving of oneself. Jesus Christ is that kind of partner; He gives more than words – He gives Himself (see Gal. 1:4).

FURTHER STUDY

Acts 2:42-47;
3:6-8;
3:11-16

1. How did God work with the apostles?

2. What did the apostles acknowledge?

He empowers! The disciples, prior to Pentecost, were afraid that they might not be able to continue the work that He had committed to them, but after receiving the gift of the Spirit all that was changed. They were like men ablaze. Peter was clearly conscious that Jesus had teamed up with them for he said, 'what I have I give you' (Acts 3:6), and you cannot give what you do not have. You have Jesus and He has you. What better partner could you find in earth or in heaven?

My Father and my God, that You should team up with me seems too good to be true. Yet it is too good not to be true. May my commitment to this partnership be as strong as Yours. In Jesus' name. Amen.

Not 'mine' but 'ours'

FOR READING & MEDITATION – 1 CORINTHIANS 3:10-22

'All things are yours, whether ... the world or life or death or the present or the future' (vv21-22)

For one more day we reflect on the idea of ordering our day on the basis of a divine partnership. I began this section by saying that this idea came from a Welsh miner who told me that every day, following his quiet time, he would think of what he had to do that day and picture Jesus involved in every moment of it. 'I am in partnership with God,' he said, 'and I have learned to think of the responsibilities of the day not as "mine" but as "ours".' This lifestyle is one that I adopted many years ago and it has brought countless spiritual benefits.

For example, as I wrote my autobiography I found myself praying prayers such as this: 'Lord, what shall we do about that situation which happened so long ago ... shall we include it or exclude it?' And, 'Lord, there is a memory here that is somewhat fuzzy and unclear. Will You help to bring it more closely into focus?'* The result is that as I write I sense God is looking over my shoulder, restraining me from writing some things and nudging me to include others that my self-protective defences might lead me to leave out.

FURTHER STUDY

2 Sam. 5:9-10, 17-25

1. Why did David become powerful?

2. How did David overcome opposition?

I do, though, feel strangely prompted to write this: somewhere in my readership today there is someone struggling to come to the right decision concerning an issue that affects your family life. Stop now and talk to Jesus along these lines: 'Lord, what shall we do about this? My life and all I am is Yours. We are partners together on the road of life. I need Your guidance and Your enlightenment. Help me. Clarify things to me please.' Why struggle through on your own when you have a partner who knows all things?

Gracious Lord, thank You that You are willing to team up with me and guide me through all of life's complicated circumstances. And Your partnership does not override my personality but strengthens it. I am so grateful. Amen.

* Selwyn Hughes, *My Story* (CWR, 2006).

Every reason to praise

FOR READING & MEDITATION – PSALM 22:1-11,19-28

'Yet you are enthroned as the Holy One; you are the praise of Israel.'

(v3)

It is time now to explore yet another way in which we can heighten our awareness of God's presence in our lives: taking the time to cultivate a praising heart. Our reading for today reminds us that the Almighty delights to dwell in the midst of His people's praise. On the basis of this verse I can promise you that the more you cultivate a praising heart, the more deeply you will feel the Lord's presence in your life. This has been true for me throughout all the days of my Christian life – and for countless other Christians that I have corresponded with also.

FURTHER STUDY

Psa. 35:28;
51:15;
1 Pet. 2:4-10

1. What are we to declare?

2. When should we praise God?

Some might object to the phrase 'cultivate a praising heart' on the grounds that they believe praise should always be spontaneous and reactive; not something that is summoned from within the soul. Therefore it might be helpful if we were to begin by differentiating between the terms praise and thanksgiving. Although thanksgiving is a close relative of praise, the two are quite distinct. We thank God for what He does and we praise Him for who He is.

The psalmist in Psalm 100:4 says, 'Enter his gates with thanksgiving and his courts with praise; give thanks to him and praise his name.' Clearly, when we come before God we are expected to bring both thanks and praise. I know some may grumble, 'I can't think of anything for which to give thanks,' but to those who feel this way I would gently suggest that they 'think again.' There is always a reason to be thankful because we have been redeemed through the innocent suffering of Jesus our Lord. And there is always a reason to give praise because God never changes. So think and give thanks, ponder and give praise.

My Father and my God, give me the insight I need to see that because of who You are I am never without a reason to praise. May my lips and my life combine today to praise and glorify Your name. Amen.

Praise is a choice

FOR READING & MEDITATION – PSALM 42:1-11

'My soul is downcast within me; therefore I will remember you' (v6)

Praise, unlike thanksgiving, originates not so much in the feelings as in the will. We can choose to praise God whether we feel like it or not. The psalmist, in the verse we have read today, is obviously feeling sad and distressed and seems to find nothing in life for which he can be thankful. But look at how he deals with his downcast state of mind.

First he recognises and admits to feeling downcast. He doesn't dwell too long on his feelings, but he is careful not to deny them. One of the greatest errors in the Christian Church is the thought that we must never admit to feeling down because once we do we have given the devil the right to take control of our lives. I have no hesitation in saying that this is simply not true and has no support in Scripture.

FURTHER STUDY

Psa. 43;
Heb. 13:10-15

1. Where would the psalmist go to praise God?

2. Where can we go?

After recognising his feelings the psalmist makes a choice: 'I will remember You from the land of the Jordan, And from the heights of Hermon, From the Hill Mizar' (v6, NKJV). He chooses to focus his thoughts not on the fact that he is feeling downcast, but on the goodness of God in bringing His people into the promised land. In the final verse of the psalm, he affirms a truth that every one of us would do well to focus on when we feel downcast: 'Hope in God; For I shall yet praise Him, The help of my countenance and my God' (vII, NKJV).

So here's a solution that it has taken me a lifetime to learn: whenever you feel sad or depressed, acknowledge your feelings and then decide by an act of your will to focus your thoughts upon the goodness of God. Learn this now and I promise you it will help save you from protracted days of sadness in the future.

Lord Jesus, I see that I will go through more times of sadness and gloom than I need to if I do not know the correct way to deal with them. Help me to learn this lesson that I have been meditating upon today – and learn it well. Amen.

'Inner health made audible'

FOR READING & MEDITATION – PSALM 147:1-20

'Praise the LORD. How good it is to sing praises to our God,
how pleasant and fitting to praise him!' (v1)

Our thoughts are concentrated at the moment on the importance of cultivating a praising heart. A doctor once told me that the happiest and healthiest people are those who are quick to praise – not the flatterers or the insincere, but those who look for and quickly recognise the praiseworthy aspects of life. He was speaking about natural things, but as I listened to him the thought came to me that if this is true in the natural arena then how much more true will it be in the spiritual arena. C.S. Lewis defined praise as 'inner health made audible'.* What did he mean? I believe he meant

FURTHER STUDY

Matt. 5:11-12;
Acts 16:16-34

1. How did Paul and Silas respond to problems?

2. What was the result?

that there is a connection between a readiness to praise and the state of our physical health.

If there really is this connection then how can it be explained? One answer, I think, is that we are made in our innermost beings for praise. God designed us to be praising beings. And there is no surer way of completing and fulfilling ourselves than giving praise – we are doing the very thing for which we were designed. Regular readers will be familiar with these words from the *Westminster Shorter Catechism*: 'Man's chief end is to glorify God and to enjoy Him for ever.' If we decide not to make it our chief occupation to praise God (and remember that to give praise is a choice we can make) then inevitably we are reduced spiritually and physically.

A Christian physician said, 'When I go through my day praising God, my blood flows better in my veins.' Praise is good for you – it not only glorifies God but it makes you a better person. So fill your life with praise knowing that this will cause God's heart to rejoice and may also be beneficial to your own heart.

Gracious and loving heavenly Father, these words of the old hymnist express everything that is in my heart: 'Fill Thou my life, O Lord my God, in every part with praise, that my whole being may proclaim Thy being and Thy ways.' Amen.

*Reflections on the Psalms by CS Lewis © copyright CS Lewis Pte Ltd 1958.

Making praise a habit

FOR READING & MEDITATION – PSALM 150:1-6

'Let everything that has breath praise the LORD.
Praise the LORD.' (v6)

Let's review what we have been saying over these past few days: there are many reasons why we praise God, not the least being the fact that when we do, we increase our awareness of His presence in our lives. How is this so? Because the Lord inhabits the praises of His people (see Psa. 22:3, ASV). Praise is the ramp down which God comes running into our hearts. We resonate so much in praise that when we reach out to Him in worship then, providing the praise and worship is genuine and not a covering up and pretence, He just cannot stay away.

Can I ask you to determine right now that you will make it a daily habit to spend some time in praise of God? Once you have made that commitment then decide how you will carry it out. Don't, whatever you do, leave it to the vagaries of feeling. A friend of mine sets his watch to bleep every hour and he uses the time signal to prompt him to focus his thoughts on praising God. Another friend who does a great deal of driving uses the moments when he is brought to a halt by a red traffic light to direct praise to God. And one minister known to me, whose telephone rings frequently, pauses for ten seconds before answering it and uses those seconds to offer adoring praise. You might say these practices are mechanical. My friends tell me that what they have chosen to do only sounds mechanical – they have found it to be medicinal.

We pick up bad habits all too quickly. As we have discovered, if we do something for thirty days it can establish itself as a habit. What is wrong with establishing a habit that enables us to turn our minds towards the Lord and give Him the praise, which He so wondrously deserves?

FURTHER STUDY

Psa. 146:1-10;
Phil. 4:4

1. List 10 things for which the psalmist gives praise.

2. Why should we always rejoice in the Lord?

My Father and my God, help me build into my life the daily habit of praise. And help me also to regard praise not merely as a duty but also as a delight. In Jesus' name. Amen.

A lesson in praise

FOR READING & MEDITATION - PSALM 63:1-11
'Because your love is better than life, my lips will glorify you.' (v3)

Dr W.E. Sangster once preached a sermon on the theme 'What eternity is too short for'. It was inspired, he said, by the experience of a minister who went to preach in a church he had never been to before and was told that partially sighted and blind people always occupied the front pews. He thought it might be encouraging if they selected a hymn with some comforting, familiar verses. Their choice of song challenged him immensely:

FURTHER STUDY

Psa. 30:1-12;
66:16-20

1. Why did the psalmist praise God?

2. What does God not withhold from us?

When all Thy mercies, O my God, my rising soul surveys,
Transported with the view, I'm lost in wonder, love, and praise.
Through all eternity to Thee, a joyful song I'll raise:
But O! Eternity's too short to utter all Thy praise.*

When the minister first looked at the blind members of the congregation, he had seen only limitations, but their positive, rejoicing hymn choice reminded him about the importance of a praising heart. The more ready we are to praise, the more aware we will be of the divine presence. Each one of us has limitations or difficult circumstances to deal with, and the best way for us to manage these issues is by opening our hearts more fully to God through praise.

If you are finding cultivating a lifestyle of praise difficult, remind yourself of these amazing truths: God is the one who truly satisfies, who upholds you and keeps you. His love is indeed 'better than life' (v3). As you begin to dwell on His goodness, your soul will become thirstier for Him. Today, open your life, and your lips, to God afresh; be thankful for His mercies and great love for you.

Father, I realise that a praising heart provides an open doorway for You to come to me, but let that not be the only reason for my praise. I praise You because of who You are - a loving and wondrous Creator. In Jesus' name. Amen.

* Joseph Addison, 1712

Truth in the inner parts

FOR READING & MEDITATION - 2 CORINTHIANS 13:1-14

'For we cannot do anything against the truth, but only for the truth.'
(v8)

Again we move on and consider a further step we can take to heighten our awareness of God's presence in our lives: break decisively with all known sin. Nothing blunts the awareness of God's presence in our lives as much as continuing to think or act in ways of which God cannot condone. If we harbour moral wrong then we are treating God as if He were unreal.

In a church over which I once had the spiritual oversight, there was a man who seemed to carry the sense of God's presence with him everywhere he went. People would often say that to spend a few minutes with him was a spiritual tonic. While visiting him in his home one day I asked him to share with me the secret of his deep spirituality. At first he was reluctant to discuss it, but after gentle probing he told me that although he had a daily quiet time, early every Sunday morning he would get alone with God and examine his life in the light of five pointed questions: (1) Have I been truthful and honest? (2) Have I been impure? (3) Have I allowed bitterness to take root in my heart? (4) Has love been my motive in everything? (5) Have I sought God's glory – or my own glory?

FURTHER STUDY

Psa. 51:6;
Eph. 4:17-25;
6:14

1. What are we to put on?

2. What are we to put off?

Take the first question: Have I been truthful and honest? How do you and I stand in the light of that searching question today? You see, truth is inviolable. The Early Christians, standing before tribunals with their lives in the balance, could have told a lie which would have saved their lives. They refused, for they knew that truth is inviolable. They could die but they could not lie. Can you be depended on to tell the truth – no matter what the cost?

God, make me from this moment on a transparent person with nothing covered - nothing that I feel the need to conceal from myself or others. You ask for truth in the inner parts. Help me to be honest in all things. In Jesus' name. Amen.

'Make me pure – but not yet'

FOR READING & MEDITATION – 1 CORINTHIANS 6:12-20

'you were bought at a price. Therefore honour God with your body.'
(v20)

For a few more moments we think about the question we started to consider yesterday: Have I been truthful and honest? How easy it is to be generous with the truth, even for a Christian? So often we are willing to stretch a meaning to gain a point, to misquote if the misquotation serves an end, to exaggerate in order to impress. What could be behind this looseness with the truth? All too frequently we believe a lie is justifiable. But it is not. We remind ourselves once again of the importance of the truth.

FURTHER STUDY

Phil. 4:8;
2 Pet. 3:1-14

1. What are our minds to dwell on?

2. For what purpose should we make every effort?

Let's look now at the second question that my friend put to himself during his weekly hour of self-examination: Have I been impure? The question of purity is fundamental; if our life flounders at this point it will probably flounder all down the line. This matter of purity seems to be an increasing problem in today's Church. Many Christians are in danger of settling for secular standards rather than scriptural ones. I remember needing to address a church official on one occasion with some evidence of serious impurity. As he threw himself down into the chair in front of me he said, 'I may be guilty, but I am still a decent man. I am not a man of the gutter.' While nobody is pure and we all stumble at times, we need to be quick to confess and return with a dependent attitude and heart.

This is a good moment perhaps to look into our own hearts and ask: Am I a pure person? Do I allow my mind to dwell on things that blunt my awareness of Jesus' presence in my life? If so, then repent of that tendency now. Don't adopt the attitude of St Augustine, who once prayed along the lines of, 'Lord, make me pure, but not just yet.'

Lord Jesus, You who were of pure mind, pure habits, pure acts, I surrender my whole being afresh to You today. Cleanse me of anything unwholesome and make my heart a place in which You can be at home. For Your own dear name's sake. Amen.

National **Prayer** Weekend

In 2015, over 1,300 churches, groups and individuals took part in our first National Prayer Weekend. Gathering prayer requests from their neighbours, thousands of people spent a fruitful weekend in September praying for God to work in their communities.

As well as from our local Christian community, we had some amazing and unexpected prayer requests from as far as Australia, South Africa, Romania, Spain, Cornwall and the House of Commons, as well as prayer requests from a number of folk who would never usually admit to having a church connection!

Following on from the encouraging feedback of last year, we want to enable and encourage individuals, groups and churches to continue to reach out to their communities through prayer, changing people's lives by encountering God. Therefore the date has now been set for another National Prayer Weekend to be held on the **23–25 September 2016**.

If you have any feedback from your 2015 National Prayer Weekend, or would like to join in and find out more about the **National Prayer Weekend 2016**, please visit **www.national-prayer-weekend.com**

No bitterness

FOR READING & MEDITATION - HEBREWS 12:12-29

'See to it that no-one misses the grace of God and that no bitter root grows up to cause trouble and defile many.' (v15)

Today we look at two more of the questions asked by my friend during his Sunday morning period of self-examination. The third question is: Have I allowed bitterness to take root in my heart? Of all the things that poison spiritual life and growth, bitterness is probably the most devastating. Jesus and bitterness are incompatible. If you hold on to bitterness you cannot hold on to Jesus, and if you hold on to Jesus you cannot hold on to bitterness. It is as simple as that. Each of us must ask ourselves at this very moment: Am I a bitter person? Do I hold grudges? Do I find it hard to forgive? If so, then surrender your bitterness now into the hands of Jesus. Give up your bitterness before it causes trouble, both to yourself and to others.

FURTHER STUDY

1 Cor. 13:1-13;
1 Pet. 4:8;
1 John 3:23-24

1. How does love overcome bitterness?

2. How can we experience the presence of Jesus?

The fourth question my friend asked himself was this: Has love been my motive in everything? All the motives of life, if they are sound, are reduced to one – love. And this love is not a general love but a specific one – the love of Christ. Paul said, 'the love of Christ controls us' (2 Cor. 5:14, RSV). This cuts deep. It is possible to be controlled by the love of achievement, of success, of a cause, of having our own way. To be controlled by the love of Christ is different, not only in degree, but in kind and quality.

When we do everything for the love of Jesus, the mundane is transformed into the meaningful, the servile into the sacred. Perhaps this, more than any other single thing, makes us aware of God's presence in our hearts. This is what the apostle John said: 'And this is his command: to … love one another … Those who obey his commands live in him, and he in them' (I John 3:23–24).

Father, enable me to face the challenge of loving and forgiving that has been presented to me today. Show me that I must do more than hear - I must obey. Please help me, dear Father. In Jesus' name. Amen.

'A little girl's first lie'

FOR READING & MEDITATION - 1 CORINTHIANS 10:23-33

'So ... whatever you do, do it all for the glory of God.' (v31)

The last question we consider is this: Have I sought God's glory – or my own glory? This, too, cuts deep. In the final analysis, what prompts your actions – self-interest or Christ-interest? Who has the final word – you or Jesus? For you see, the issue is this: if you control your life then Jesus cannot permeate it. You will not feel His presence as strongly in your heart. You will be more self-conscious than Christ-conscious.

Although these five questions helped sharpen my friend's spiritual life I am not suggesting that they should be used repeatedly by everyone. It is possible that Jesus may lead you in a different direction. What is important, however, is that we are willing, from time to time, to expose ourselves to some form of self-examination or spiritual review. Many of us have regular physical check ups, and wouldn't dream of ignoring the results or recommendations. To review our lives and position in relation to God and decide *not* to do something about the things we discover are affecting our spiritual awareness could cause great difficulty.

A young girl went into a guest's room and stole some sweets. When challenged by her mother as to where she got them, she told her first lie. Her mother explained why it is wrong not to tell the truth. The little girl cried in response and her mother said, 'I'm glad to see you're sorry – now take the sweet out of your mouth and throw it away.' Through her tears the little girl looked at her mother, clamped her mouth shut and then said, 'No, I'm enjoying it too much.' She refused to do the one thing that was necessary – give it up.

FURTHER STUDY

Col. 3:1-10, 17, 23-24

1. What should captivate our mind?

2. What attitude should we have to work and life?

Father, if ever I needed Your help it is over this matter. Save me from just identifying the things that dull my awareness of Your presence in my life; help me to give them up also. In Jesus' name I pray. Amen.

Christian fellowship

FOR READING & MEDITATION – MATTHEW 18:15–20

'For where two or three come together in my name,
there am I with them.' (v20)

Once again we move on and consider yet another way of increasing our awareness of God's presence in our lives. This is one that almost every Christian can pursue except perhaps those who are somehow isolated through no fault of their own. I refer to the joy of meeting together in fellowship with other Christians. Most of us do this, but not all of us understand the significance of what happens when we meet together in Jesus' name.

Although the presence of Jesus is with every Christian, whenever we meet together corporately for prayer and worship His presence seems to be felt more intensely by each of us individually. Why should this be? One reason, I think, is this: in the process of opening up our spirits to one another we open ourselves more fully to God. This is something that has intrigued me for many years, for I have discovered that the more effort I make to relate to my brothers and sisters in Jesus, the closer I seem to get to God. It is as if in the physical presence of other Christians – as we pray together, sing together and share together – somehow that opens our spirit more completely to God.

FURTHER STUDY

Acts 11:25-30;
12:5;
19:8-10;
20:7

1. What was the practice of the early disciples?

2. What happened at their gatherings?

C.S. Lewis once expressed a similar thought in these words: 'God can show Himself as He really is only to ... men [and women] who are united together in a body, loving one another, helping one another, showing Him to one another ... consequently the only really adequate instrument for learning about God is the whole Christian community, waiting for Him together.'* The closer we get to each other the closer we will get to God, and the closer we get to God the closer we will want to get to each other.

Father, I am so grateful for the fellowship I have with other Christians. Help me to cherish that and to enjoy its benefits in my personal life and experience. For Jesus' sake. Amen.

*Mere Christianity by CS Lewis © copyright CS Lewis Pte Ltd 1942, 1943, 1944, 1952.

What makes a fellowship?

FOR READING & MEDITATION - JOHN 17:20-26

'I pray also for those who will believe in me through their message,
that all of them may be one' (vv20-21)

Today we pursue the thought that meeting together with other Christians is one of the most effective and fun ways of experiencing God's presence. The idea we considered yesterday – that the more we open up to each other the more we open up to Jesus – is something that we ought to be more aware of and pay more attention to in the contemporary Christian community. You see, if we do not take the necessary steps to develop authentic relationships then we inevitably deprive ourselves of the joy of experiencing His presence as a body of believers. God can mediate His presence in and through a community of His people only to the extent that they are open to Him and to one another.

In a number of churches known to me the people have a common tradition, subscribe to a common creed, share a common form of doctrine, but do not belong to each other. They think that sharing common beliefs makes them a living fellowship but it does not. What makes a group of Christians a living fellowship is their desire and willingness to open up to one another; 'do' life together and share at the deepest level. Children who do not feel they belong in a family are usually troubled children. It is the same with the family of God.

What is the situation in your church? Do you feel it is a place where you really belong – belong not just to Jesus but to one another? If so, then rejoice in this. If not, then begin to share yourself with your brothers and sisters as fully as you are able. When those who belong to a church have no true relationship with each other, a barrier is formed that blocks the way for the mediation of God's presence to the whole body of believers.

FURTHER STUDY

Acts 2:37-47;
Phil. 1:3-5;
1 John 1:7

1. To what did the early disciples devote themselves?

2. For what was Paul thankful?

Father, I see that if the members of a local church are not in harmony with one another then the power of Your presence is limited. Bless my own fellowship this day and make us truly one. In Jesus' name I pray. Amen.

Things that hinder

FOR READING & MEDITATION - 1 CORINTHIANS 11:23-34
'But if we judged ourselves, we would not come under judgment.'
(v31)

For a further day we stay with the thought that when those who belong to a church do not pay attention to the need to deepen their relationships with each other then they will not experience a keen sense of God's presence in their midst. God can mediate His presence only to the degree that His people are willing to open themselves up to Him and to each other. One exception to this, as far as I know, is during a period of revival, when God flows into a community with such amazing and awesome power that He sweeps aside all obstacles and hindrances.

FURTHER STUDY

Lam. 3:40;
Matt. 7:1-5;
1 Pet. 4:17

1. Where does judgment begin?

2. Why do we see others' faults but not our own?

Some time ago I heard of a church where the leaders and the congregation, recognising that they were not experiencing Jesus' presence in their meetings as fully as they should, got together one Saturday for a time of self-examination. As they shared openly with one another it became obvious that there were many barriers between them. They were courageous enough to identify the things that divided them and make a list of them: fears, suspicions, jealousies, resentments, guilt, self-preoccupation, a desire to have one's own way, resistance to God-given authority and so on.

The list was displayed using an overhead projector and the acknowledgement made: 'These are the things that keep us from one another.' Someone then asked, 'What shall we do?' The decision was made to separate into small groups and devote several hours a week to the task of building better relationships. It was a cleansing process – a catharsis. Then what happened? I am sure you will have guessed: God made His presence felt so powerfully in their midst that they entered into a new dimension of spiritual authority and power.

Heavenly Father, I pray that around Your world today Your children might come to see the importance of being more open to one another and to You. Begin with me, dear Lord. In Jesus' name I ask it. Amen.

Meeting in Jesus' name

FOR READING & MEDITATION - HEBREWS 10:19-39

'Let us not give up meeting together ... but let us encourage
one another' (v25)

We should not get the impression from what we have been saying that all we need to do to realise Jesus' presence among us is to relate to each other. This would put the focus on us, and not on Him.

One of the issues that can arise in churches where there is a strong relational focus is that people concentrate more on the horizontal relationships than on the vertical relationship. We must never forget that it is in Jesus' name that we meet. No matter how good our horizontal relationships, if we lose sight of the fact that we are to focus more on Him than on ourselves we will never experience His presence to our fullest potential. After all, what gives a Christian congregation cohesion? It is the presence of Jesus in their midst. How different Christian communities would be if we focused more on the thought that we are not just a group of compatible people getting together but are in reality meeting together with the living God.

Many years ago, when I was pastor in Yorkshire, I used to visit an elderly lady who would always remark as I bade her farewell by her garden gate, 'I will see you at the next meeting, for I don't want to miss meeting Him.' Most people would have simply said, 'I will see you at the next meeting.' This lady's focus, however, was not on meeting with other Christians; it was on meeting with her Lord. She loved 'them', but she loved 'Him' even more. In our times of fellowship our priorities are to be in that order – first 'Him' and then 'them'. Linking ourselves first with 'Him' and then with 'them' is one of the greatest means we have of experiencing the presence of God.

FURTHER STUDY

Matt. 18:20;
2 Cor. 8:1-5;
1 John 1:1-4

1. Where do we find Jesus?

2. How are vertical and horizontal relationships revealed?

My Father and my God, help me not to get this matter out of focus and make more of meeting with my brothers and sisters than of meeting with You. In every gathering I long to meet You. Amen.

'Feelings from nowhere'

FOR READING & MEDITATION - PSALM 23:1-6

'he restores my soul. He guides me in paths of righteousness
for his name's sake.' (v3)

Having seen how the indwelling of the Holy Spirit increases our awareness of God's presence in our lives we turn our attention now to the arena of our thinking and feelings. Did you know that wrong attitudes and unrestored hurts can affect you to such a degree that they can actually suppress the sense of God's presence within your soul?

When I entered the Christian ministry (more decades ago than I care to remember) I found that, despite my theological training, there were some people whom I could not help. They were the ones who came to me and said something along these lines: 'I know I am a Christian, but there are times when God's presence seems to leave me and I am overcome by feelings of deep loneliness and sadness. I have asked God to forgive my sin and I am not conscious of anything in my life that is dishonouring to Him. These feelings seem to come out of nowhere and without any apparent reason. I am unsure what I should do about them. Can you help me?'

FURTHER STUDY

Ruth 1:1-20

1. Why was Naomi depressed?

2. What was her view of God?

When faced with such a situation I don't mind telling you that I was completely and hopelessly lost. Then I stumbled upon the solution: some of these people were feeling this way because of some unresolved hurt from the past, some unsettling memory that had been repressed or some unhealthy attitude that had never been corrected. From time to time these matters returned to trouble them and blunted their spiritual sensitivity and sense of joy.

If you have ever experienced the type of problem I am talking about then I hope that what we will unpack together over the next few days will help and equip you to deal with it whenever it occurs again.

My Father and my God, help me to come to You that I might learn not only to keep my body under control but also my mind and my emotions. This I ask in Jesus' peerless and precious name. Amen.

Inner wounds

FOR READING & MEDITATION – PROVERBS 18:1-14

'A man's spirit sustains him in sickness, but a crushed spirit
who can bear?' (v14)

Yesterday we said that some people's awareness of God
is at times blunted by uncharacteristic, debilitating and
even terrifying feelings that can arise within them and affect
their spiritual sensitivity, depriving them of joy. Such people
can be walking along the street with a deep awareness of
Jesus' presence in their life when, without warning and for
no apparent reason, a dark cloud descends upon their soul
and dampens their emotional and spiritual mood. Often the
cause of this is that something from that person's past – a
repressed fear, perhaps, or an unresolved hurt or a serious
rejection – has intruded into the present, taking its
toll on the personality.

Some time ago a person said to me, 'There are
times when I feel God's presence surrounding me
so closely that I feel like dancing with joy, and
then suddenly, for some reason, I feel incredibly
lonely. Why is this?' Circumstances prevented me
spending much time with this person, but a few
carefully constructed questions brought us both to
understand that there was a wound in that person's
spirit that had never fully healed.

But what is a wounded spirit? We usually think
of wounds occurring in battles or during a fight,
but the spirit too can be wounded, and such wounds are
sometimes deeper and more painful than a physical wound.
The wounds I am talking about here usually arise from one
of two things: serious hurts or deep horrors. The hurts come
from rejection or being deprived of love. The horrors come
from having experienced trauma, brutality, violence and
physical abuse. Can Jesus really sympathise and help us
with our deep inner wounds? I want to reassure you that
He can and He does.

FURTHER STUDY

Ruth 4:9-17;
2 Cor. 12:9-10;
Heb. 4:15-16

1. How was
Naomi
restored?

2. How can
we deal with
difficulties?

**Lord Jesus, it was said of You that You were wounded in the
house of Your friends. Now Your wounds speak to my wounds.
Please heal me of any inner hurt or horror that may be troubling
me. In Your name I ask it. Amen.**

Emotional healing

FOR READING & MEDITATION – PHILIPPIANS 1:1-11

'he who began a good work in you will carry it on to completion until the day of Christ Jesus.' (v6)

In some Christian circles – thankfully, not all – whenever the matter of past problems intruding into the present is mentioned, the objection is raised: 'What are you doing? Are you denying the power and reality of conversion? All those things are dealt with at the moment a person is converted – why hark back to the past?'

One thing that has caused great difficulty in the Christian Church is the thought that conversion instantly resolves all our emotional problems. This simply is not true. Some people *are* instantly healed of all their emotional problems, but generally, while we are made anew and given a fresh start, we still need to deal with and work through the consequences of our past. We cannot begin to help each other until we are willing to face reality and realise that some things are not as we would like them to be. But how is a wounded spirit healed? What can we do to begin to overcome the consequences of the past that sometimes intrude into the present and blunt the edge of our spiritual awareness?

FURTHER STUDY

Rom. 15:1;
Gal. 6:2-5;
James 5:13-16

1. What should we do if we are strong?

2. What should we do if we are troubled?

First, we need to accept the fact that these things are going on within us. Don't hide from them and say, 'All matters from the past were dealt with at my conversion.' This kind of difficulty cannot be dealt with by wishful thinking, so acknowledge it to yourself and, if you can, share it with another Christian – or maybe, if necessary, a counsellor. Many years ago I would not have given this advice, but experience has shown me that many Christians miss out on healing because they are unwilling to open up and share a particular matter with another person.

Father, in this quest for health – inner health as well as physical health – make me completely realistic and willing to face up to everything. This I ask in Jesus' name. Amen.

Bring it to God

FOR READING & MEDITATION - JOHN 5:1-15

'When Jesus saw him lying there ... he asked him,
"Do you want to get well?"' (v6)

Yesterday we began to consider the steps we should take when things from our past intrude into the present and dampen our experience of God's presence. The second step we can take is to accept some responsibility for the way we are. But you say, 'I was the one who was rejected, deprived and subjected to the most debilitating and damaging trauma.'

It is true that we cannot always affect and choose the things that happen to us in life. We can, however, with God's help, love and tender grace, choose the manner of our response to what happens. While this is naturally counter-intuitive – and for a while painfully and deeply difficult – it is utterly liberating. With God's help it is possible: He specialises in open-heart surgery, which can help you forgive and release yourself and those who may have hurt you in the past.

FURTHER STUDY

Gen. 37:23-28;
50:15-21

1. How did Joseph feel towards his brothers?

2. Why could he be so forgiving?

Third, we ask ourselves if we really want to be healed and delivered. This is what Jesus asked the man who had been ill for thirty-eight years: 'Do you want to get well?' It is possible for past problems to serve a purpose for us. One purpose might be to get sympathy from others. Another purpose could be to use the hurts we have received as an excuse to hurt others.

The fourth step that must be taken is to bring whatever is troubling you to God and ask Him to heal and restore it. If you are careful to go through the other three measures I have recommended, this last step will be a very natural one. If you feel that nothing has changed then go over the first three steps again because something is being missed. Whenever we place our trust in God, He is always faithful and true.

Yes Lord, I want to be whole. Help me renounce all my wrong choices and wrong attitudes. Sweep through my inner being with the breath of Your Spirit and deliver me from all that binds me to the past. In Jesus' name I pray. Amen.

Sharing - an inherent impulse

FOR READING & MEDITATION - 2 CORINTHIANS 5:12-21
'For Christ's love compels us, because we are convinced that
one died for all' (v14)

We continue reflecting on the different ways by which we can sharpen our awareness of God's presence in our lives. Another way is to ensure that we give out what God puts in. I call this the discipline of sharing. We need to learn to be intentional and look for opportunities to share by word and deed what we know of God as we are about praying and reading the Scriptures.

Many of us fail to do this. We are earnest and regular in our quiet times but have not disciplined ourselves to share. A special event or a serious conversation may prompt us to

FURTHER STUDY

Acts 8:1-4;
1 Cor. 9:16-23

1. How did persecution cause the Church to flourish?

2. How did Paul adapt his message for everyone?

share. But this kind of sharing is more by accident than by choice; it is a question of occasion rather than a question of intentional will. The natural impulse of a heart in which God's love and presence dwells is to radiate that love and presence to others.

Perhaps you have already heard the story of the man who, finding a little dog by the roadside with a broken leg, took it to his house and attended to it until the leg had healed. As soon as its leg was better the dog began to run around the house, and then one day it disappeared. The man had grown to love the little dog and felt somewhat disappointed and deserted. The following day, however, the dog he had cared for was back again, but this time there was another little dog with it – and the other little dog was lame! The impulse in that dog's heart was natural and right – it was the impulse to share what it had received with others.

Does God's love and presence abide deeply in you? Great. But be aware of this: when you take the initiative and share that love with others it will grow even deeper and richer, and sharing will become a natural way of life.

Father, who can feel Your love and power stirring in their heart and not want to share it? The impulse is there - inherently. Help me not to choke it. In Jesus' name. Amen.

No freedom without law

FOR READING & MEDITATION - PSALM 119:1-16

'Blessed are they who keep his statutes and seek him with all their heart.' (v2)

We continue our discussion on intentional giving and sharing. Just in case it has not occurred to you already, the point needs to be made: experiencing the presence of God involves a certain amount of discipline. Some of the measures I am suggesting in this issue require deliberate and concentrated effort. It is much easier to relax and let things happen of their own accord, but I have observed that it is the disciplined and intentional who make things happen.

No doubt there are some who will object and say, 'We have been made for freedom. All this talk about discipline is an anathema to Christianity.' But freedom only comes through disciplined obedience. I am free from pressure by the police only as I obey the law; within the framework of the law they enforce I am free. Someone has expressed it like this: 'I am free to swing my arm, but my freedom ends at the tip of your nose.' There is no such thing as absolute freedom; freedom, if it means anything at all, is controlled and confined by law. And it is a law of the kingdom of God that what flows into the soul must pass through the soul. Intake must result in outflow.

FURTHER STUDY

Rom. 8:1-13; Gal. 5:1,13-16

1. What law are we free from?

2. What law are we to follow?

I once heard a preacher say, 'God is like electricity: He won't come in unless He can get out.' Well, that is not quite true, but I am sure you understand his illustration. God is not interested in just living in us; He is interested also in living *through* us. The amazing thing about sharing with others what God has graciously imparted to us is that we become all the better for the sharing. As we give so we receive. And not only do we become better – we become better off. We experience His presence in a more real and wonderful way.

Gracious Father, I have been influenced by too many things. I have obeyed this and that and the result is that I have become this and that - nothing. Please help me to be a disciplined person. In Jesus' name I pray. Amen.

Don't be a hearer only

FOR READING & MEDITATION – REVELATION 22:1-21

'The Spirit and the bride say, "Come!" And let him who hears say, "Come!"' (v17)

Consistently over the years, both in letters and in private conversation with other Christians, I have been presented with this question: 'Although I have known the presence of God in my life in a real and vital way, now, for some reason, it seems to have ebbed away. Why is this?' There are numerous possible reasons why this might happen – an unforgiving spirit, neglect of prayer and the reading of God's Word, or even a physical disorder – but I have found that most frequently the cause is that the person concerned has failed to share what he or she knows of God with others.

FURTHER STUDY

John 4:19-30;
James 1:22-25

1. How did the woman respond to meeting Jesus?

2. Why may we be deceived?

If there is no outflow, the inflow automatically dries up. It is a law of life that whatever is not used atrophies – it dies.

Professor Henry Drummond, in his book *Natural Law in the Spiritual World*, talks about some fish caught in the dark waters of the Mammoth Caves in Kentucky, USA. It was found that although these fish had eyes, they could not see. No one quite knows how they got into the caves, but there in the darkness where no natural light ever penetrated eyesight became superfluous. 'Nature,' said Professor Henry Drummond, 'adopted the position – what you don't use, you don't need.'

Now, of course, we cannot push this too far and suggest that if we do not share God's love and presence with others we will lose our salvation, because that is not what Scripture teaches. It is a fact, however, that the more we share what we have received, the more we will have to share. Today's verse challenged me greatly in my youth. When I read it the Spirit said to me, 'You have been a hearer – now say "Come!"' I went out and led my first person to Jesus.

Lord God, I long to always be at my best for You. Help me to turn from being just a 'hearer' to someone who bids others 'come'. In Jesus' name I pray. Amen.

FOR READING & MEDITATION - JOHN 1:35-51

'Philip found Nathanael and told him, "We have found the one
Moses wrote about in the Law"' (v45)

Many people are hesitant to share the love and presence of God with others because they are not sure how to go about it. I dislike distinctly the idea of 'selling religion' because it buys into commercialism and consumerism, and makes Jesus into something else to be consumed. Nevertheless, there are some things we can learn from those whose task it is to sell products.

In my experience with sales people, I have noticed that the ones who make an impression usually do so for two basic reasons. One is that they present as though the thing they are selling is of great importance to them, and two, they do not push too hard, for they know this might produce an unfavourable reaction. I once heard a sales manager give four steps in presenting a product: (1) What is it? (2) What will it do for you? (3) Who says so? (4) How can you get it? I commend these four steps to those of you who struggle in sharing with others what God has shared with you.

What is it? First clear away misconceptions and help someone understand what being a Christian is not. It is not being joined to a religion but being joined to a Person. What will living for and following Jesus do for you? You will find forgiveness, freedom, reality, a sense of inner unity and of 'coming home'. Who says so? Jesus does through His Word and through the testimony of multitudes of His followers. How can you get salvation? By repenting of sin – not just wrong habits and actions but the basic sin of self-dependence – depending on self rather than on God. I recommend these four questions as a basic framework for sharing Jesus with others.

FURTHER STUDY

Acts 26:16-20;
Rom. 10:8-17

1. How do people come to faith?

2. What was Paul's calling?

My Father and my God, all around me, on radio and television, I hear the witness to false gods - the gods of materialism and pleasure. Help me to witness all the more clearly to You. In Jesus' name. Amen.

Affirmative praying

FOR READING & MEDITATION – PSALM 107:1-22

'Let the redeemed of the LORD say this – those he redeemed from the hand of the foe' (v2)

Another thing we can do to help sharpen our awareness of God in our lives is to pray in the affirmative way. Although there are many series and books on prayer, few emphasise the importance of praying affirmatively. Nevertheless, the concept underlying this is, I believe, a biblical one. Praying in the affirmative way is not asking for something to be so but affirming that it is so; it is proclaiming that a matter is exactly the way God has decreed it. You see, there are some things in the Christian life that we do not need to ask for at all – they are part and parcel of God's provision for us as His children. And the promise of God's continued presence is one of them.

FURTHER STUDY

1 Chron. 29:10-13; Acts 4:23-30

1. Compare these prayers.

2. Why are affirmative prayers important?

Earlier we looked at a number of verses from Scripture that confirm this, such as 'Never will I leave you; never will I forsake you' (Heb. 13:5). This verse and others – and indeed there are many more – give us the guarantee that once we surrender our lives to God and are His committed sons and daughters then His presence will be in and around us every moment of the day. So do not ask for it, affirm it. Instead of praying, 'O God, be with me through every moment of this day,' say, 'Thank You, Father, that You are with me right now.' Where once you may have prayed, 'May Your presence always surround me,' say, 'Thank You, Father, that I am always surrounded by Your presence; You are in me, around me, above me, beneath me, behind me, in front of me.'

Psychologists say that affirmation has a powerful effect and helps to bring the whole personality to health. It is not wishful thinking to say that God is with you. It is the affirmation of a great and wonderful biblical truth.

Gracious Father, every day I need to learn more of the Christian way. If there is something that I need to discover then let there be an inner witness in my heart. In Jesus' name I ask it. Amen.

True believing

FOR READING & MEDITATION – PSALM 91:1-16

'He who dwells in the shelter of the Most High will rest in the shadow of the Almighty.' (v1)

Yesterday we said that there are some things in the Christian life that we do not need to ask for – they are part and parcel of God's provision for us as His children. And the continued presence of Jesus Christ in our lives is one of them. Concerning some things in life, we would have to say in all honesty that we are not sure if we know the mind of God about them. Thus before we can proceed we pray and petition Him for light and illumination. But no Christian need be unsure of God's promise to dwell in the hearts of those who are His children. He has put the issue beyond all possible doubt by assuring us, as we see from today's text, that He is always with us.

Why, then, do we find ourselves so often praying for God to be with us instead of simply affirming it? I have thought long and hard about this and I believe that basically there are two reasons why we do this. One is that when we come into the Christian life we hear others pray this way and, without thinking, we follow suit. The other is that deep down in our hearts we have not been gripped with the assurance that what God has said in His Word about being with us is really true. Unless this becomes a deep conviction then, when adverse conditions develop, we will be left wondering if He is still with us.

Opinions are something we hold; convictions are something that hold us. So drop your anchor into the depths of this reassuring and encouraging revelation, and never again raise the anchor: God is with you always. Let the truth pass from being an opinion into a firmly held conviction. Behind it lies all the authority of heaven.

FURTHER STUDY

Psa. 27:1;
46:1-11;
John 14:23

1. How can we know and affirm God's presence?

2. What is Jesus' promise to us?

Gracious and loving Father, I do not want to rationalise Your promises; I want to realise them. Help me to examine my motives and see whether, deep down, I really believe what Your Word tells me. Amen.

'Simply believe'

FOR READING & MEDITATION – PSALM 139:1-12

'Where can I go from your Spirit? Where can I flee from
your presence?' (v7)

Today we carry on considering that when we ask God to give us His companionship, even though He has already pledged to do so, this may be a sign of our struggle to believe. Is this too hard a statement? I think not. It is far better to acknowledge that this is a possibility and consider it than to dismiss it out of hand. So ask yourself now: Do I believe that Jesus' presence is with me every moment of the day? If your answer is 'Yes' then ask yourself this further question: Then why do I not affirm it more frequently?

Another reason why we might not pray in this affirmative

FURTHER STUDY

Exod. 33:14;
Isa. 43:1-7

1. What is God's commitment to us?

2. How does He see us?

way is because we do not understand the difference between the prayer of petition and the prayer of affirmation. To petition God is to ask Him for something and to keep on asking until He answers that prayer by giving us one of the following responses: an affirmative 'Yes', 'No' (because what we are asking for is not good for us), 'Later, at a more appropriate time' or, 'I will give you something better.' To affirm something is to acknowledge that God wants to give us what we desire and all we have to do is to open ourselves

to it. We do not have to plead with God that we might experience His presence; we simply have to affirm it.

Answer these questions in your heart right now: Do you know without any shadow of doubt that God wants you to experience His continued presence in your life? And is His presence limited to a certain hour or part of the day? The answer to the first question is 'Yes' and to the second 'No.' There is no need to constantly ask God for His presence. The matter is settled for ever. So don't pray for it; affirm it and be strengthened and courageous in His company today.

Dear Father, I see that I do not have to ask for Your presence – I already have it. In You I live and move and have my being. Thank You that You are with me everywhere I go. I am eternally grateful. Amen.

NEXT ISSUE

Seek Me and Live

In this verse-by-verse exploration of the prophecy of Amos, our Father's heart is revealed in how He directly warns and challenges the hypocrisy and corruption of the nation of Israel.

The message given to Amos is both challenging and reassuring, highlighting God's love of justice and opposition of the oppression of the poor. Whilst a forgiving Father, He will not stand by inactive and watch His people living lives based on selfishness and greed.

God's heart is that we seek Him and Live.

Every Day
with Jesus

JUL/AUG 2016

'let justice roll on like a river, righteousness like a never-failing stream'
Amos 5:24

Seek me and live

Be revived and refreshed by God's Word   CWR

Also available as eBook/ eSubscription

OBTAIN YOUR COPY FROM
CWR, a Christian bookshop or National Distributor.
If you would like to take out a subscription, see the order form at the back of these notes.

Growing in faith

FOR READING & MEDITATION – MARK 11:12-25

'Therefore I tell you, whatever you ask for in prayer, believe that you have received it, and it will be yours.' (v24)

For one more day we discuss the difference between the prayer of petition and the prayer of affirmation. The truth is that when it comes to the matter of the presence of God, we need not petition Him at all. It may seem, as we said, that we are taking His presence for granted, but really this is not the case. We are simply taking God at His Word.

Some might think all this is a quibble about words, and will say, 'What does it matter how we frame our prayers? God knows what we mean. After all, a loving earthly father would not get upset with a child who phrases his statements incorrectly. A father's love overlooks all that.'

FURTHER STUDY

John 11:38-40;
17:13;
Acts 27:21-26

1. How did Jesus use affirmation in His prayers?

2. What was the basis of Paul's affirmation?

That is quite true, but this needs to be looked at not so much from God's side but from ours. You see, the statements of Scripture that show God's presence is always with us require of us a degree of faith, and exercising faith, generally speaking, is not something we are very good at doing. We would much prefer not to have to exercise faith and believe that God means what He says, and instead pray using words such as these: 'Lord, help me to believe that Your presence is with me everywhere I go.'

I know full well that there are times when we have to pray like that, for instance, when our faith is weak and we are going through a hard and difficult time. What I am advocating, however, is exercising our faith so that more and more we begin to take God at His Word. If we can't affirm something that the Lord has made crystal clear in the Bible – His constant presence – then how are we going to grow in faith so that we can affirm those things that are not so clear?

Father, forgive me that so often I shrink from the challenge to increase my faith. It is so much easier to ask for things than to believe for them, but I want to grow. I know how to petition – please teach me now to affirm. Amen.

The breath of God

FOR READING & MEDITATION - JOB 33:1-18

'The Spirit of God has made me; the breath of the Almighty
gives me life.' (v4)

We continue our exploration of the ways in which we
can sharpen our awareness of God's presence in our
lives. Another suggestion I would make is to establish simple
daily practices that help to remind us of the fact that He
is constantly with us. Earlier on, I referred to the idea of
establishing habits that remind us of the need to praise,
but now I would like to talk about establishing some habits
that will help to remind us of the nearness of our Master's
presence. These practices might not appeal to everyone,
but those who follow them say they have greatly helped
in bringing about a sharper awareness of God's
presence in their lives.

Dr Frank Laubach, a medical practitioner
who made a lifelong study of the methods that
Christians follow to increase their awareness of
God's presence, said that the following are some
of the most popular: walking on the inside of the
pavement and visualising Jesus walking on the
kerb side; playing the game of 'Minutes' in which
you see how many times during an hour you think
of God and then counting the number of minutes
that you thought about Him; taking a breath and
saying, 'As this breath of air I am taking is filling
my whole body with life-giving oxygen so the breath of God,
when I take it in, strengthens and sustains my inner life.'

A friend of mine says that this last suggestion is one that
he sometimes follows – taking slow, steady breaths while
sitting quietly in God's presence and using that as a focus
to remind him that the Almighty is closer than the very air
we breathe. My suggestion is that right now you pause for
a moment of quietness, take a few deep breaths and say the
following prayer:

**My Father and my God, as this breath of air I am taking is cleansing
the blood in my lungs from all impurities, so Your breath, as I
take it within my being, purifies my inner life. I am so very, very
grateful. Amen.**

FURTHER STUDY

Job 32:6-8;
Psa. 33:1-6;
119:164

1. What does
the breath of
God achieve?

2. What was the
daily habit of
the psalmist?

Staying alert

FOR READING & MEDITATION - PROVERBS 25:11-25

'Like cold water to a weary soul is good news from a distant land.'
(v25)

Our Lord Jesus who, during His ministry here on earth, used many graphic images – in His parables, for example – understands better than anyone how physical things can be used to increase spiritual awareness and understanding. I confess that for many years I viewed some of the practices people have developed to help them remember how close God is to them as nothing more than 'crutches' needed only by those who would not give priority to daily Bible reading and prayer. As I have talked with devout Christians about their spiritual lives, however, I have had to change my mind about this. I have seen how, in addition to regular Bible reading and prayer, the establishing of a simple daily habit has made their relationship with God even more meaningful.

FURTHER STUDY

2 Kings 9:17-20;
Isa. 62:6-7;
Matt. 26:36-41

1. What are the duties of a watchman?

2. Why is it important to stay alert?

We think now about another practice used by some in order to remind themselves of God's continuing presence in their lives: being alert and watching for anything interesting or unusual that happens during the day, and immediately bringing God into it. One woman I know who does this explains, 'Whenever something unusual or unexpected happens in my day, such as bumping into a friend I haven't seen for years or receiving a surprise phone call or gift, I immediately relate the happening to God, and say, "Lord, how lovely of You to arrange my day in this way." I have done this so often that now it has become a fixed habit – one that immediately focuses my mind on His all-pervading presence.'

Stay alert and watch out for the unusual and the unexpected today – and allow it to trigger an awareness and appreciation of Jesus' constant presence in your life.

Gracious and loving heavenly Father, I realise that there are many things I can do to increase my awareness of Your presence in my life. Help me to choose the ones that are best for me. In Jesus' name. Amen.

'You are always on my mind'

FOR READING & MEDITATION - PSALM 139:1-24

'Before a word is on my tongue you know it completely, O LORD.' (v4)

Another way of increasing the sense that God is present in your life is, as the writer David Benner puts it, *to attend to God's attention to you*. In other words, reflect on the fact made clear in our text for today that God is constantly watching over us and thinking about us.

Some time ago, inside my Saturday morning paper I found a free CD entitled *The 40 Greatest Love Songs Ever*. I decided to listen to them. Although many were not my kind of tunes on this occasion there was one that caught my interest. It was a song first made popular by Elvis Presley but being covered by Willie Nelson: *You are Always on My Mind*. The song – a kind of lament – is about a man who does not treat his wife in the way he should and one day comes to see how foolish he has been. As I listened to it there came singing into my consciousness a number of verses from the Bible that tell us about God's constant attention to His children. From what we are told in the text before us today and many other scriptures it is possible, I believe, to affirm what God says concerning us, 'You are always on My mind. I am always thinking about you.' How wonderful to know that the great God who created the universe thinks about His children continuously.

A businessman who is frequently away from home says, 'I can't tell you how comforting it is to know that many times during the day my wife is thinking of me.' Well, God thinks about you not only many times during the day but every moment of the day. And attending to His attention to you is a wonderful way of increasing your awareness of His presence in your life.

FURTHER STUDY

Psa. 40:1-5;
Jer. 29:10-14;
Eph. 1:3-11

1. Why are we on God's mind?

2. What are God's thoughts and plans for us?

Father, how awesome is the fact that Your attention is always on me. I take comfort from the thought that I am never out of Your mind. Help me attend to Your attention of me. In Jesus' name. Amen.

The divine mind

FOR READING & MEDITATION - ROMANS 11:33-36

'Who has known the mind of the Lord? Or who has been his counsellor?' (v34)

Yesterday we started to think about God's attentiveness to us, His much loved children. The divine mind is so vast, so profound that He can think of every one of His children at the same time. And His care and concern for us, I believe, extends to the tiniest details of our lives.

Just before beginning this page I remembered something that happened when I was leading a tour to the Holy Land. During the drive from Jerusalem to Galilee – a journey of several hours – I sat next to a young woman who every so often would look at her watch, close her eyes and stop conversing with me. Eventually I asked her what she was doing and she replied, 'I have a pact with my boyfriend that whenever we are separated we think of each other for a whole minute on the hour and every half hour.' I thought this was quite sweet and it led to a conversation about how God thinks about us not on the hour or half hour but every single moment of the day. Though some may find this difficult to understand, God's thoughts about His children are not infrequent, occasional or sporadic. He thinks about us continuously.

The psalmist in Psalm 139:18 tells us that God's thoughts are more in number than the grains of sand on the seashores of the world. And the same thought that has gone into the construction of the created world has gone also into the plan of salvation. This might be speculation on my part but I imagine that God thinks about His redeemed children more than He does about the material universe. To create the world He simply spoke, but to save us He had to give His one and only Son to die on a cross. The humblest soul means more to Him than a million galaxies.

FURTHER STUDY

Isa. 55:6-13;
1 Cor. 2:9-16

1. Compare God's thoughts and our thoughts.

2. How can we know God's thoughts?

Father, how attentive You are to the needs and concerns of Your children. May my attentiveness to Your attentiveness serve to deepen my sense of Your presence in my life. In Jesus' name. Amen.

'All coheres in Him'

FOR READING & MEDITATION – COLOSSIANS 1:1-20

'He is before all things, and in him all things hold together.' (v17)

For some the idea that God thinks about us every moment of the day is almost unbelievable. They find it incredible that the great God who created this universe watches over His children and that His attention is never drawn away from them.

Some time ago I listened to the wife of a famous British celebrity who, when asked if she believed in God, said, 'Yes, I believe in a Creator but I don't believe in a God who takes a personal interest in His creatures.' Theologians have a term to describe this idea – Deism. It's the belief that God created the universe and wound it up like a clock and then went away and let it run all by itself. The text before us today disproves this idea. It reveals that not only did God create the universe through Jesus but also that He is the One who holds it together. To use the words found in the Moffatt translation, 'all coheres in him'. Jesus is involved in His creation and takes a personal interest in every aspect of our daily lives. We may not attend to Him but He most certainly attends to us. A man once said to me, 'Do you really believe that the great Creator notices your presence in the midst of this vast universe?' I was glad to tell him that I did, and that the reason why I did was, to quote the old chorus, 'He walks with me and talks with me and tells me I am His own.'

Though God's thoughts, understanding and wisdom are far above our thoughts, we dare to believe on the authority of His Word that His thoughts are always directed towards His children. Though worlds move at His word, it is not the mountains or the stars or the galaxies that He thinks about, but you and me. Blessed be His holy name for ever.

FURTHER STUDY

John 1:1-10; Heb. 1:1-3

1. How are creation and salvation linked?

2. How did the world respond to its Creator?

Loving Father, the idea that I am continuously in Your thoughts is something that I would have difficulty believing were it not written in Your Word. Help me to live this day in the truth of this amazing news.

Never forgotten

FOR READING & MEDITATION – ISAIAH 49:8-15

'Can a mother forget the baby at her breast … ? Though she may forget, I will not forget you!' (v15)

I f I understand Scripture correctly there is not a moment when God's eyes are off me or His attention is distracted from me. I am never out of His mind.

Some time ago the media reported the visit of a famous footballer to a boy who was dying. Apparently the boy was a great fan of the footballer and so when he visited him he gave him the gift of a football with his signature on it. The press were present to take photographs and the footballer was applauded by all for his apparent concern. Some months later the same footballer was asked by a member of the press about the child he had visited who was so seriously ill. The footballer looked blank and confessed that he had forgotten all about his visit to the dying boy. Had it all just been a publicity stunt? Some seemed to think so.

FURTHER STUDY

Isa. 44:21-23; Jer. 31:20,33-34

1. What will the Lord never forget?

2. What will the Lord never remember?

In terms of your relationship with God that will never happen to you. You have the assurance that He will never forget you. Others may forget you – they may forget your birthday, they may forget an anniversary, they might even forget your name after a while – but God will never forget you. I happen to believe that the most exciting thing about my life is not that I know God but that He knows me. Of course, I am excited that I know Him, but I am more excited by the fact that He knows me. And why? Because my knowledge of Him is based on His knowledge of me. If He didn't know me then I would never have come to know Him. I once made that remark – that my knowledge of God is based on His knowledge of me – to a woman and she subsequently said it changed her life. I hope it does the same for someone reading these lines today.

Father, help me draw comfort from the thought that though others may forget me, You will never forget me. I will always remain in the centre of Your thoughts. Thank You once again, my Father. Thank You. Amen.

Think about it

FOR READING & MEDITATION – MATTHEW 6:25-34

'Look at the birds of the air; they do not sow or reap ...
and yet your heavenly Father feeds them.' (v26)

We began this section by saying that one of the many ways of increasing our awareness of God's presence in our lives is to attend to His attention to us. But how does that work in practice? Like this: what we think about greatly affects the way we feel. It is a simple law of psychology that our thinking influences our feelings and leads to decisions made by the will. People often say to me, 'I know God loves me, but I don't feel it very often.' Then think more about the fact that He does.

Martyn Lloyd-Jones, in his writings on the Sermon on the Mount, talks about faith and asks this question: 'What is faith?' Let's pause for a moment to think. How would you define faith? This is what Lloyd-Jones says: 'Faith ... is primarily *thinking*.' He quotes the words of Jesus found in today's reading and points out that here Jesus is saying, 'Look at the birds, *think* about them and draw your deductions. Look at the grass, look at the lilies of the field, *consider* them'. After years of Christian experience I can tell you that the more I think about how God thinks about me, how much He loves me and how much I mean to Him, the more my thoughts affect my feelings, and in those feelings His presence can be felt.

If you are one of those people who never feels the love of God sweeping into your soul then the remedy is in your own hands. Consider the verses of Scripture that talk about His love and His personal interest in you. Ponder them. Think about them. Thinking will open the door of your soul to a deeper awareness of His presence. Sometimes when I think about how God thinks about me tears begin to fill my eyes.

FURTHER STUDY

Job 37:14;
Psa. 8:3-4;
Luke 12:24-28;
Heb. 12:1-3

1. What things should we think about?

2. What can we learn from nature?

Lord Jesus, forgive me that I spend so much of my time thinking about the wrong things. Help me to think more about the things that I ought to think about – the things that speak to me of Your unceasing care and love. Amen.

Ending each day with God

FOR READING & MEDITATION – PSALM 63:1-11

'On my bed I remember you; I think of you through the watches of the night.' (v6)

Now we come to the last of my suggestions for increasing our awareness of God's presence in our lives: end every day with a few minutes' reflection on your experience of God during the waking hours.

For centuries this simple practice has been called the *examen* – a daily examination of the conscience. However, it is my belief that although the examination of the conscience and the confession of sin are important, the examen can go beyond the conscience to consciousness itself. The ultimate goal is to transform our consciousness by increasing our awareness of God's presence. 'When blessed by God,' says one writer, 'the examen is a discipline that holds within the possibility of transforming our experience of God, both conscious and unconscious.'

FURTHER STUDY

Gen. 24:62-67;
Psa. 141:1-2

1. What did Isaac do in the evening?

2. Why should we pray in the evening as well as the morning?

Those who have written on the examen in the past say it is best made by putting a fence around a few minutes at the end of the evening (ten minutes at least). Begin by imagining yourself in the presence of Jesus and in dialogue with Him. Thank Him for the day and His presence in it. Then ask for His help in seeing the day from His point of view. This is best done by imagining yourself watching the day with Jesus and letting the things of the day pass quickly as from a fast-forwarded DVD. Your prayer is to let Jesus stop 'the DVD' and allow Him to interrupt your stream of consciousness and focus on those parts of the day that warrant reflection.

The goal of the exercise is to observe how aware you were of God's presence in those moments. If you were not aware of His presence what was blocking it? God is present every moment of our day. What is sad is that so often we don't expect to find Him.

My Father and my God, help me not to take each day for granted. Forgive me if I overlook Your involvement in my life. Please help me to become increasingly aware of Your presence. In Jesus' name. Amen.

'Centring prayer'

FOR READING & MEDITATION - ECCLESIASTES 9:1-10

'Whatever your hand finds to do, do it with all your might' (v10)

The exercise we are talking about now – the examination of consciousness at the end of the day – was, as far as we can tell, first introduced into Christian practice by St Ignatius, who described it in his book *Spiritual Exercises*. Our text today tells us that whatever our hand finds to do, we should do it with all our might. The examen is something that needs to be made with diligence and attentiveness. The rewards, however, are out of all proportion to the time it takes.

I have found that one of the greatest spiritual difficulties people have is sitting still in the presence of God and listening to what He has to say. When I was a young man, my pastor gave me some advice that helped me overcome this difficulty. He told me, 'Whenever you find your mind drifting then simply say the name of Jesus and it will bring you back on track.' This has worked for me and I know it has worked for thousands more with whom I have shared his advice. Sometimes this is called 'centering prayer' – a subject that is wonderfully dealt with by Basil Pennington in his book by the same title.

Proficiency in the art of the examen comes through practice so don't expect too much in the first few days. When you become aware that you thought God was absent in a certain situation that occurred ask Him to help you discern that in reality He was present. We learn, I believe, to understand that whatever happens God can turn to good. Often we are angry and frustrated when He doesn't deliver us from certain situations and feel He cannot have been there. We learn that, though things happen, God's plans and purpose will ultimately prevail. He sees, knows and understands a bigger plan that includes not just us but others as well.

FURTHER STUDY

2 Kings 6:8-17;
1 Cor. 11:28-31;
2 Cor. 13:5

1. How may situations change when we examine them with God?

2. Why should we examine ourselves?

Father, I have come far in my Christian walk but there is still much for me to learn. I long to discern more of Your presence in my life. Yet I see that this will not happen automatically. Help me do what is required of me. Amen.

The perfect end to a day

FOR READING & MEDITATION - PSALM 119:145-152

'My eyes stay open through the watches of the night, that I may meditate on your promises.' (v148)

Those who recommend ending the day with an examination of consciousness (of whom I am one) say that we should always be ready to do two things in particular. One is to share with Jesus our sorrow that we were not more aware of His presence, and the other is to pray for His help in being more aware of His presence in the day that is to come.

The first time I engaged in this practice I was struck by the realisation that I had already been conscious of God's presence but had not focused on it. You might well find the same. When I started to focus on His presence, however, I gained a tremendous sense of joy and strength from the knowledge that I was always in His presence and that His eye was always upon me. Honesty compels me to admit, though, that at first the daily spiritual exercise was frustrating as it brought home to me the fact that I was relying to a great extent on my beliefs and not on experience. From the early days of my Christian life I had been taught to forget about experience and concentrate on beliefs. 'You are what you believe,' I was told, 'and if you look to experience you may well be disappointed.' Now I have come to see that this advice, though given with good intentions, was flawed. In attempting to direct me away from seeking to experience God, my spiritual advisors had deprived me of something that would have been of great benefit to my soul.

With absolute certainty I can say that the practice of reviewing God's presence at the end of the day has meant as much to me as any other spiritual exercise I have undertaken, and has helped me not only deepen my faith in God but to experience Him more deeply also.

FURTHER STUDY

Psa. 77:1-12; 119:52-56

1. What did the psalmist specifically remember?

2. What was his practice?

My Father and my God, Your presence in my heart means more to me than anything. A deeper sense of that presence is what I long for more than words can convey. Once again, I pray, help me play my part. In Jesus' name. Amen

The still small voice

FOR READING & MEDITATION - 1 KINGS 19:9-18

'the LORD was not in the fire. And after the fire came
a gentle whisper.' (v12)

For one more day we focus on the suggestion of ending the day with God in the examen. One preacher was concerned that he experienced God only when he was preaching, through the sense of empowerment he felt when expounding the Word of God to his congregation. When he discussed this with someone who had been a Christian for many years, this is what he was asked: 'Are you expecting God to make His presence known in the same way under all circumstances? If so you are missing the deep sense of His presence because you are looking for Him only in the wind and the fire and not in the still small voice.'

The preacher confessed that his constant prayer was, 'Lord, give me power in my ministry, anoint my preaching, help me to feel Your presence as I open up Your Word to Your people.' His difficulty, he came to see, was that he expected God to come to him only in feelings of power – the feelings he experienced when he was ministering the Word. He was advised to close his eyes and sit quietly and listen to what the Spirit was saying to him right there and then. 'Just listen,' said his advisor, 'and don't worry about saying anything in response.' He closed his eyes and prayed, 'Speak Lord, Your servant is listening.' After a few minutes he opened his eyes wide and said, 'God has just spoken to me.' 'What did He say?' asked his spiritual advisor. 'He told me He loved me,' said the preacher. That one moment changed the entire course of his life from that day forward.

Have you ever prayed that prayer and sat still for a while in God's presence? There is nothing more wonderful than not only feeling His presence but hearing His voice in your soul also.

FURTHER STUDY

Isa. 30:21;
Matt. 3:13-17

1. When might we hear God's voice?

2. What did the voice say even before Jesus' ministry began?

Father, I see that my expectations play an important part in this exercise of increasing my awareness of Your presence in my life. May my expectations become greater and greater, I pray. In Jesus' name. Amen.

Practice makes perfect

FOR READING & MEDITATION - PSALM 16:1-11

'You have made known to me the path of life; you will fill me with joy in your presence ' (v11)

On this our last day together we ask: What are some of the benefits that flow from an increased awareness of God's presence in our lives? The first benefit is that it makes us stronger in faith. The more we realise that by the simple act of remembering we can sharpen our awareness of God's presence in our hearts, the more easily we will be able to put our faith into operation in the bigger issues of our lives.

The second benefit is that it makes us stronger in hope. 'Hope grows in proportion to our knowledge,' said Brother Lawrence of the Resurrection hundreds of years ago, 'And according as our faith penetrates through this holy exercise [reminding ourselves that God's presence is constantly with us] into the secrets of the Divine ... our hope grows and strengthens itself, and the grandeur of the blessing that it desires, and in some manner already tastes, satisfies and sustains it.' A third benefit is that it makes us stronger in love. The more we gaze upon God, the more we will love Him, and, of course, the converse is also true – the more we love Him, the more we will gaze upon Him.

FURTHER STUDY

Psa. 17:6-15; 27:4-5

1. What would satisfy the psalmist?

2. What did the psalmist seek first and foremost?

The more willing we are to take measures to experience His presence, the more acutely we will feel His presence. So remember that you are not alone. At the time of seeming aloneness, He is closer to you than you realise. But do not take His presence for granted. He has said He will never leave you or forsake you, but we need to constantly remind ourselves of that fact. Like all things in life – practice makes perfect. So go out now and from this time forward determine to experience God's presence in your life to a greater extent than you have ever done before.

Lord God, help me to put into practice the things You have taught me. As the hours come and go may they be beautified by Your presence to a degree I have never known before. In Jesus' name I ask it. Amen.

ORDER FORM

4 EASY WAYS TO ORDER:

1. Phone in your credit card order: **01252 784700** (Mon-Fri, 9.30am - 5pm)

2. Visit our online store at **www.cwr.org.uk/store**

3. Send this form together with your payment to:
   CWR, Waverley Abbey House, Waverley Lane, Farnham, Surrey GU9 8EP

4. Visit your local Christian bookshop

a list of our National Distributors, who supply countries outside the UK, visit www.cwr.org.uk/distributors

YOUR DETAILS (REQUIRED FOR ORDERS AND DONATIONS)

Full Name:	CWR ID No. (if known):
Home Address:	
	Postcode:
Telephone No. (for queries):	Email:

PUBLICATIONS

TITLE	QTY	PRICE	TOTAL
		Total publications	

All CWR adult Bible-reading notes are also available in eBook and email subscription format.
Visit www.cwr.org.uk for further information.

UK p&p: up to £24.99 = **£2.99**; £25.00 and over = **FREE**

Elsewhere p&p: up to £10 = **£4.95**; £10.01 - £50 = **£6.95**; £50.01 - £99.99 = **£10**; £100 and over = **£30**

Please allow 14 days for delivery | **Total publications and p&p A** | |

SUBSCRIPTIONS* (NON DIRECT DEBIT)

	QTY	PRICE (INCLUDING P&P)			TOTAL
		UK	Europe	Elsewhere	
Every Day with Jesus (1yr, 6 issues)		£15.95	£19.95	Please contact nearest National Distributor or CWR direct	
Large Print *Every Day with Jesus* (1yr, 6 issues)		£15.95	£19.95		
Inspiring Women Every Day (1yr, 6 issues)		£15.95	£19.95		
Life Every Day (Jeff Lucas) (1yr, 6 issues)		£15.95	£19.95		
Mettle: 14-18s (1yr, 3 issues)		£14.50	£16.60		
YP's: 11-15s (1yr, 6 issues)		£15.95	£19.95		
Topz: 7-11s (1yr, 6 issues)		£15.95	£19.95		
Cover to Cover Every Day		Email subscription only, visit online store.			
Total Subscriptions (Subscription prices already include postage and packing) **B**					

ease circle which bimonthly issue you would like your subscription to commence from:
an/Feb Mar/Apr May/Jun Jul/Aug Sep/Oct Nov/Dec

Only use this section for subscriptions paid for by credit/debit card or
cheque. For Direct Debit subscriptions see overleaf.

CONTINUED OVERLEAF »

PAYMENT DETAILS

☐ I enclose a cheque/PO made payable to CWR for the amount of: **£** _____

☐ Please charge my credit/debit card.

Cardholder's Name (in BLOCK CAPITALS) _____

Card No. ☐☐☐☐ ☐☐☐☐ ☐☐☐☐ ☐☐☐☐ ☐☐☐☐

Expires End ☐☐☐☐   Security Code ☐☐☐

GIFT TO CWR ☐ Please send me an acknowledgement of my gift   **C** ☐

GIFT AID (YOUR HOME ADDRESS REQUIRED, SEE OVERLEAF)

giftaid it

I am a UK taxpayer and want CWR to reclaim the tax on all my donations for the four years prior to this year **and on** all donations I make from the date of this Gift Aid declaration until further notice.*

Taxpayer's Full Name (in BLOCK CAPITALS) _____

Signature _____ **Date** _____

*I understand I must pay an amount of Income/Capital Gains Tax at least equal to the tax the charity reclaims in the tax year.

GRAND TOTAL (Total of A, B, & C) ☐

SUBSCRIPTIONS BY DIRECT DEBIT (UK BANK ACCOUNT HOLDERS ONLY)

Subscriptions cost £15.95 (except *Mettle*: £14.50) for one year for delivery within the UK. Please tick relevant boxes and fill in the form

☐ *Every Day with Jesus* (1yr, 6 issues)
☐ Large Print *Every Day with Jesus* (1yr, 6 issues)
☐ *Inspiring Women Every Day* (1yr, 6 issues)
☐ *Life Every Day* (Jeff Lucas) (1yr, 6 issues)

☐ *Mettle*: 14-18s (1yr, 3 issues)
☐ *YP's*: 11-15s (1yr, 6 issues)
☐ *Topz*: 7-11s (1yr, 6 issues)

Issue to commence
☐ Jan/Feb ☐ Jul/Aug
☐ Mar/Apr ☐ Sep/Oct
☐ May/Jun ☐ Nov/Dec

CWR

Instruction to your Bank or Building Society to pay by Direct Debit

DIRECT Debit

Please fill in the form and send to: CWR, Waverley Abbey House, Waverley Lane, Farnham, Surrey GU9 8EP

Name and full postal address of your Bank or Building Society

To: The Manager _____ Bank/Building Society

Address _____

_____

_____ Postcode _____

Name(s) of Account Holder(s) _____

Branch Sort Code ☐☐ ☐☐ ☐☐

Bank/Building Society Account Number ☐☐☐☐☐☐☐☐

Originator's Identification Number

4	2	0	4	8	7

Reference
☐☐☐☐☐☐☐☐☐☐☐☐☐☐☐☐☐☐

Instruction to your Bank or Building Society
Please pay CWR Direct Debits from the account detailed in this Instruction subject to the safeguards assured by the Direct Debit Guarantee.
I understand that this Instruction may remain with CWR and, if so, details passed electronically to my Bank/Building Society.

Signature(s) _____

Date _____

Banks and Building Societies may not accept Direct Debit Instructions for some types of account